EASY
Thai

EASY
Thai

Learn to Speak Thai Quickly

Jintana Rattanakhemakorn

TUTTLE Publishing

Tokyo | Rutland, Vermont | Singapore

The Tuttle Story: "Books to Span the East and West"

Many people are surprised to learn that the world's largest publisher of books on Asia had its humble beginnings in the tiny American state of Vermont. The company's founder, Charles E. Tuttle, belonged to a New England family steeped in publishing.

Immediately after WWII, Tuttle served in Tokyo under General Douglas MacArthur and was tasked with reviving the Japanese publishing industry. He later founded the Charles E. Tuttle Publishing Company, which thrives today as one of the world's leading independent publishers.

Though a westerner, Tuttle was hugely instrumental in bringing a knowledge of Japan and Asia to a world hungry for information about the East. By the time of his death in 1993, Tuttle had published over 6,000 books on Asian culture, history and art—a legacy honored by the Japanese emperor with the "Order of the Sacred Treasure," the highest tribute Japan can bestow upon a non-Japanese.

With a backlist of 1,500 titles, Tuttle Publishing is more active today than at any time in its past—inspired by Charles Tuttle's core mission to publish fine books to span the East and West and provide a greater understanding of each.

Published by Tuttle Publishing, an imprint of Periplus Editions (HK) Ltd.

www.tuttlepublishing.com

ISBN: 978-0-8048-4256-3

Library of Congress CIP data in progress.

First edition
18 17 16 15
10 9 8 7 6 5 4 3 2 1   1411MP

Printed in Singapore

Distributed by

North America, Latin America & Europe
Tuttle Publishing
364 Innovation Drive, North Clarendon,
VT 05759-9436, USA
Tel: 1 (802) 773 8930; Fax: 1 (802) 773 6993
info@tuttlepublishing.com
www.tuttlepublishing.com

Japan
Tuttle Publishing
Yaekari Building 3rd Floor, 5-4-12 Osaki
Shinagawa-ku, Tokyo 1410032, Japan
Tel: (81) 3 5437 0171; Fax: (81) 3 5437 0755
sales@tuttle.co.jp; www.tuttle.co.jp

Asia Pacific
Berkeley Books Pte Ltd
61 Tai Seng Avenue #02-12,
Singapore 534167
Tel: (65) 6280 1330; Fax: (65) 6280 6290
inquiries@periplus.com.sg
www.periplus.com

Indonesia
PT Java Books Indonesia
Jl. Rawa Gelam IV No. 9
Kawasan Industri Pulogadung
Jakarta 13930, Indonesia
Tel: 62 (21) 4682 1088; Fax: 62 (21) 461 0206
crm@periplus.co.id; www.periplus.com

Contents

Introduction 7
- The Thai script
- Consonants, vowels, and tones

LESSON 1: ## Greetings 13
- Greetings and introductions
- Asking someone's name and nationality
- Talking about what you can and can't do

LESSON 2: ## Food 27
- Talking about food
- Ordering a meal in a restaurant
- Food, drink, and cooking vocabulary

LESSON 3: ## Family 43
- Talking about family members
- Numbers
- Talking about occupations

LESSON 4: ## What time is it? 57
- Telling the time
- Talking about daily routines

LESSON 5: ## Yesterday and tomorrow 73
- Talking about past events
- Talking about future plans
- Leisure activities vocabulary

LESSON 6: ## Shopping 83
- Shopping dialogues
- Everyday items, color, and size vocabulary

LESSON 7: Directions 95
- Asking and giving directions
- Locations vocabulary

LESSON 8: How are you today? 105
- Talking about feelings

LESSON 9: Health 115
- Describing ailments
- Parts of the body
- Responding to advice

LESSON 10: Describing people 125
- Describing appearances
- Describing personality

LESSON 11: Communications 137
- Talking on the phone
- Using the Internet
- Talking to the bank teller

Answer key 154

Thai–English Glossary 156

English–Thai Glossary 177

Introduction

The eleven lessons in *Easy Thai* contain everything the self-study learner needs for a quick, functional grasp of daily communicative Thai, without having to spend time attending language school or investing in expensive textbooks for formal study.

Each chapter focuses on a practical situation the visitor to Thailand may experience, through the character of Jim, an American who is visiting Thailand to study. As you follow Jim's adventures you'll learn how to communicate in a variety of realistic scenarios— from introducing yourself to friends and colleagues and ordering food at a restaurant to asking for help with health problems and carrying out simple transactions at the bank.

Key language for each new topic is introduced through a dialogue that presents new words and phrases in context. The dialogues are followed by a breakdown of key sentence patterns, simple grammar explanations, lists of related phrases and vocabulary, and practice exercises. An answer key for the practice exercises is provided at the back of the book. The accompanying audio CD contains recordings of all key dialogues, words, and phrases by native Thai speakers, so that you can practice correct pronunciation. A detailed pronunciation guide and information about the Thai script is also included on pages 8–11.

Along with cultural notes in every chapter, and an appendix containing glossaries of useful vocabulary, this book has everything you need to not only survive in Thailand but to enjoy interacting with the Thai people you meet and develop rewarding relationships. Happy traveling!

Jintana Rattanakhemakorn

The Thai Script

The Thai alphabet was created in 1283 by King Ramkhamhaeng and was probably derived from the Old Khmer alphabet. Thai has an alphabetic script with a few distinctive features – it has no spaces between words as well as no small and capital forms like the Roman alphabet. Each unit of the alphabetic script represents a sound.

In this book, you are primarily learning conversational Thai, but Thai script is included so that you can start to become familiar with the language in its written form. In this introductory section you will find guidelines for the correct pronunciation of each Thai vowel and consonant. Throughout the book, each time a Thai word or phrase is used, romanized pronunciation is included, using the sounds below.

The simplified set of instructions that follow will help the beginner in Thai, working alone, to achieve level of pronunciation sufficient for basic daily communication.

Thai Consonants

There are 44 consonant characters in Thai representing 20 consonant sounds. The following listing follows Thai alphabetical order. Of these 44 consonants, the two underlined are obsolete.

ก ข ฃ ค ฅ ฆ ง จ ฉ ช ซ ฌ ญ ฎ ฏ ฐ ฑ ฒ ณ ด ต ถ ท ธ
น บ ป ผ ฝ พ ฟ ภ ม ย ร ล ว ศ ษ ส ห ฬ อ ฮ

Consonant sound	Consonant form (Thai word)	Sounds like
k	กิน **_kin_**	g as in go
kh	ขา **_khǎa_**	k as in <u>k</u>ind
ng	ง **_ngou_**	ng as in si<u>ng</u>ing
j	จาน **_jaan_**	j as in <u>j</u>et
ch	ฉัน **_chǎn_**	ch as in <u>ch</u>at

Consonant sound	Consonant form (Thai word)	Sounds like
s	ซื้อ *súe*	s as in <u>s</u>un
y	ยา *yaa*	y as in you
d	เดิน *doen*	d as in do
t	เต้น *tên*	t as in stop
th	ไทย *thai*	t as in teach
n	น้ำ *nám*	n as in nine
b	บ้าน *bâan*	b as in boy
p	ไป *pai*	p as in spot
ph	พ่อ *phâw*	p as in pan
f	ฟัน *fan*	f as in fun
m	แมว *maew*	m as in man
r	เรียน *rian*	r as in rat
l	ลอง *lawng*	l as in let
w	วัด *wát*	as in win
h	หิว *hǐw*	h as in hand

0.02

Stop ending

When these consonants appear at the end of a word, they are not voiced aloud.

Consonant sound	Consonant form (Thai word)	Sounds like
k	จาก *jàak*	g as in bag
t	พูด *phôut*	d as in loud
p	ครับ *khráp*	b as in tab

0.03

Vowels

There are 18 single vowels in Thai, which appear singly or in combination. Thai vowels have two "sounds": **short** and **long**.

1. Short vowels

There are nine "short" vowels and dipthongs:

Vowel sound	Vowel form (Thai word)	Sounds like
a	จะ *jà*	a as in b<u>u</u>t
i	สิ *sì*	i as in h<u>i</u>t
ue	รื *rúe*	as o in less<u>o</u>n
u	ดุ *dù*	u as in p<u>u</u>t
e	เตะ *tè*	e as in g<u>e</u>t (shorter)
ae	และ *láe*	ae as in c<u>a</u>t (shorter)
o	โปะ *pò*	o as in <u>o</u>nly (shorter)
aw	เกาะ *kàw*	aw as in h<u>o</u>t
oe	เถอะ *thòe*	oe as in <u>uh</u>

2. Long vowels

Each of the short vowels and dipthongs above has its long counterpart. There are also two further long dipthongs, *ai* and *ao*:

Vowel sound	Vowel form (Thai word)	Sounds like
aa	ชา *chaa*	aa as in f<u>ar</u>
ii	ดี *dii*	ii as in t<u>ea</u>
ue	มือ *mue*	ue as in <u>umm</u>
ou	ปู *pou*	ou as in t<u>oo</u>
e	เท *the*	e as in l<u>a</u>te

ae	แจ *jae*	ae as in f<u>a</u>n
o	โม *mo*	o as in c<u>o</u>ld
aw	ขอ *khǎw*	aw as in s<u>aw</u>
oe	เบอ *boe*	oe as in h<u>er</u>
ai	ไจ/ใจ *jai*	ai as in h<u>igh</u>
ao	เรา *rao*	ao as in <u>ou</u>t

*Note: the letter อ in Thai can be pronounced a, e, i, o, or u, depending on the letter combination in which it appears. For example:

อ่าน *àan*	a as in at
เอ็ด *èt*	e as in egg
อิ่ม *ìm*	i as in it
อ้วน *oûan*	o as in on
อุ่น *ùn*	u as in up

0.04

Tones

Thai has only 5 distinctive tones; *mid, low, falling, high,* and *rising.* They all carry tone marks except for mid-level tones. The pitch of a particular word changes its meaning.

Thai script tone marks	Tone level	E.g, with romanized tone mark	Meaning
No mark	mid ➡	กา *kaa*	to get stuck
◌่	low ⬇	ก่า *kàa*	galangal (spice)
◌้	falling ⌢	ก้า *kâa*	I, slave, servant
◌๊	high ↗	ก๊า *káa*	trade
◌๋	rising ⎷	ก๋า *kǎa*	leg

LESSON 1

Greetings

In this lesson you will learn how to greet people, introduce yourself, and ask and answer questions about things you can and can't do.

DIALOGUE 1: *Listen and repeat*

1.01

Malee: *Sà-wàt-dii khâ. Chǎn chûe Malee khâ. Khun chûe à-rai khá?*
สวัสดีค่ะ ฉัน ชื่อ มาลี ค่ะ คุณ ชื่อ อะไร คะ
Hello. My name is Malee. What is your name?

Jim: *Sà-wàt-dii khráp. Phǒm chûe Jim khráp.*
สวัสดีครับ ผม ชื่อ จิม ครับ
Hello. My name is Jim.

Malee: *Khun Jim maa-jàak prà-thêt à-rai khá?*
คุณจิม มาจาก ประเทศ อะไร คะ
What country are you from, Jim?

Jim: *Phǒm maa-jàak prà-thêt à-me-rí-kaa khráp.*
ผม มาจาก ประเทศ อเมริกา ครับ
I am from America.

Greetings *Listen and repeat*

1.02

sà-wàt-dii khâ (female speakers)
สวัสดี ค่ะ

sà-wàt-dii khráp (male speakers)
สวัสดี ครับ

⎫
⎬ Hello
⎭

chǎn (female speakers) ฉัน		
dì-chǎn (formal, women only) ดิฉัน		I/me
phǒm (male speakers) ผม		

khun	คุณ	you
khǎo	เขา	he/she/they
rao	เรา	we
chûe	ชื่อ	name
chûe-lên	ชื่อเล่น	nickname
naam-sà-kun	นามสกุล	last name
maa-jàak	มาจาก	from
prà-thêt	ประเทศ	country
rát	รัฐ	state
jang-wàt	จังหวัด	province

1.03

Countries *Listen and repeat*

à-me-rí-kaa	อเมริกา	the United States
ang-krìt	อังกฤษ	United Kingdom
khae-naa-daa	แคนาดา	Canada
áws-tre-lia	ออสเตรเลีย	Australia
niw-sii-laen	นิวซีแลนด์	New Zealand
fà-ràng-sèt	ฝรั่งเศส	France
yoe-rá-man	เยอรมัน	Germany
ì-taa-lii	อิตาลี	Italy

rát-sia	รัสเซีย	Russia
sà-pen	สเปน	Spain
thai	ไทย	Thailand
in-dia	อินเดีย	India
jiin	จีน	China
yîi-pùn	ญี่ปุ่น	Japan
kao-lĭi	เกาหลี	Korea

PATTERN PRACTICE 1

■ What's your name?

Khun	*chûe*	*à-rai?*
คุณ	ชื่อ	อะไร
You	name	what?
	chûe-lên	
	ชื่อเล่น	
	nickname	
	naam-sà-kun	
	นามสกุล	
	last name	

■ My name is . . .

Chăn	*chûe*
ฉัน	ชื่อ
I (women)	name . . .
Phŏm	*chûe-lên*
ผม	ชื่อเล่น
I (men)	nickname . . .
	naam-sà-kun
	นามสกุล
	last name . . .

PATTERN PRACTICE 2

■ What country are you from?

Khun	*maa-jàak*	*prà-thêt*	*à-rai?*
คุณ	มาจาก	ประเทศ	อะไร
You	from	country	what?
Khǎo		*rát*	
เขา		รัฐ	
(He/she/they)		state	
		jang-wàt	
		จังหวัด	
		province	

■ I am from America.

Chǎn	*maa-jàak*	*prà-thêt*	*à-me-rí-kaa.*
ฉัน	มาจาก	ประเทศ	อเมริกา
I (women)	from	country	America.
Phǒm		*rát*	
ผม		รัฐ	เมน
I (men)		state	Maine.
Khǎo		*jang-wàt*	*Khǒn Kàen.*
เขา		จังหวัด	ขอนแก่น
(He/she/they)		province	Khon Kaen

Grammar Corner

✪ Polite particle *khá* / *khâ* / *khráp*

These words are used to end a sentence in order to make an utterance sound very polite and respectful.

*Note: throughout the book the polite sentence endings are used in dialogues, but not in the example sentences.

- The word *khâ* (for women) is used for statements, commands, and also used alone as a polite way to answer "yes."

- *khá* (for women) is used at the end of a question.
- *khráp* is a neutral ending for men to use in any situation.

Exercises

EXERCISE 1: *Listen and repeat*

1.04

Sà-wàt-dii khâ. (women) สวัสดี ค่ะ *Sà-wàt-dii khráp.* (men) สวัสดี ครับ	Hello.
Khun chûe à-rai? คุณ ชื่อ อะไร	What is your name?
Chăn (women) */ phŏm* (men) *chûe...* ฉัน / ผม ชื่อ...	My name is...
Chăn/phŏm naam-sà-kun... ฉัน / ผม นามสกุล...	My last name is...
Chăn/phōm chûe-lên... ฉัน / ผม ชื่อเล่น...	My nickname is...
Khun maa-jàak prà-thêt à-rai? คุณ มาจาก ประเทศ อะไร	What country are you from?
Chăn/phŏm maa-jàak prà-thêt à-me-rí-kaa. ฉัน / ผม มาจาก ประเทศ อเมริกา	I am from America.
Khun maa-chàak rát à-rai? คุณ มาจาก รัฐ อะไร	What state are you from?
Chăn/phŏm maa-jàak rát Maine. ฉัน / ผม มาจาก รัฐ เมน	I am from the state of Maine.

EXERCISE 2: Listen and circle the sentence you hear.

1. a. What's your name?
   b. What's your last name?

2. a. I am from America.
   b. He's from America.

3. a. What province are you from?
   b. What state are you from?

4. a. My name is Jane.
   b. My nickname is Jane.

5. a. Which country is she from?
   b. Which country are you from?

6. a. I'm from California.
   b. I'm from KhonKaen.

EXERCISE 3: Practice introducing yourself in Thai.

> Hello. My name is............... My last name
> is............... My nickname is............... I am
> from...............

DIALOGUE 2: *Listen and repeat*

Malee: **_Khun Jim phôut phaa-săa à-rai khá?_**
คุณจิม พูด ภาษา อะไร คะ
What languages do you speak, Jim?

Jim: **_Phǒm phôut phaa-săa-ang-krìt khráp._**
ผม พูด ภาษาอังกฤษ ครับ
I speak English.

Malee: ***Khun Jim phôut phaa-sǎa-thai dâi-mái khá?***
คุณจิม พูด ภาษาไทย ได้ไหม คะ
Can you speak Thai?

Jim: ***Phǒm phôut phaa-sǎa-thai dâi nít-nòi khráp.***
ผม พูด ภาษาไทย ได้ นิดหน่อย ครับ
I can speak Thai a little bit.

Malee: ***Khun Jim khǐan phaa-sǎa-thai dâi-mái khá?***
คุณจิม เขียน ภาษาไทย ได้ไหม คะ
Can you write in Thai?

Jim: ***Mâi-dâi khráp.***
ไม่ได้ ครับ
No, I can't.

1.07

Can and can't *Listen and repeat*

phôut	พูด	speak
rian	เรียน	study, learn
sǎwn	สอน	teach
khǐan	เขียน	write
àan	อ่าน	read
phaa-sǎa	ภาษา	language
phaa-sǎa-thai	ภาษาไทย	Thai language
phaa-sǎa-ang-krìt	ภาษาอังกฤษ	English language
dâi	ได้	able to
mâi-dâi	ไม่ได้	unable to
nít-nòi	นิดหน่อย	bit, little
dâi-mái	ได้ไหม	Can ....?

1.08

Languages *Listen and repeat*

Add **phaa-săa** in front of the country name (see list, pages 14–15) to make the word meaning the language of that country. For example

Country	Language
thai	**phaa-săa-thai**
ไทย	ภาษาไทย
Thailand	Thai
sà-pen	**phaa-săa-sà-pen**
สเปน	ภาษาสเปน
Spain	Spanish
jiin	**phaa-săa-jiin**
จีน	ภาษาจีน
China	Chinese

*Note: the word for "English"—**phaa-săa-ang-krìt**—does not conform to this rule.

PATTERN PRACTICE 3:

■ What language do you speak?

Khun	**phôut**	**phaa-săa**	**à-rai?**
คุณ	พูด	ภาษา	อะไร
You	speak	language	what?
	khĭan		
	เขียน		
	write		
	aàn		
	อ่าน		
	read		

■ I speak Thai.

Chǎn	phôut	phaa-sǎa-thai.
ฉัน	พูด	ภาษาไทย
I (women)	speak	Thai.
Phǒm	khǐan	phaa-sǎa-ang-krìt.
ผม	เขียน	ภาษาอังกฤษ
I (men)	write	English.
	àan	
	อ่าน	
	read	

PATTERN PRACTICE 4:

■ Can you speak English?

Khun	phôut	phaa-sǎa-ang-krìt	dâi-mái?
คุณ	พูด	ภาษาอังกฤษ	ได้ไหม
You	speak	English	can?
	khǐan	phaa-sǎa-thai	
	เขียน	ภาษาไทย	
	write	Thai	

■ I can speak English. / I cannot write in Thai.

Chǎn	phôut	phaa-sǎa-ang-krìt	dâi.
ฉัน	พูด	ภาษาอังกฤษ	ได้
I (women)	speak	English	can.
Phǒm	khǐan	phaa-sǎa-thai	mâi-dâi.
ผม	เขียน	ภาษาไทย	ไม่ได้
I (men)	write	Thai	cannot.

■ I can speak a bit of Thai.

Chăn	*phôut*	*phaa-săa-thai*	*dâi*	*nít-nòi.*
ฉัน	พูด	ภาษาไทย	ได้	นิดหน่อย
I (women)	speak	Thai	can	a little bit.

Phŏm	*khĭan*	*phaa-săa-ang-krìt*		
ผม	เขียน	ภาษาอังกฤษ		
I (men)	write	English		

Grammar Corner

✪ **Can and can't**

The term **dâi-mái** refers to (1) having the ability or skill to do something, and (2) having permission to do something. To answer "yes," say **dâi**; for "no," respond with **mâi-dâi**. These words are placed at the end of a sentence in both the question and the answer.

Example:

Questions	Yes.	No.
Khun wâai náam dâi-mái? คุณ ว่ายน้ำ ได้ไหม Can you swim?	*Chăn/phŏm wâai náam dâi.* ฉัน / ผม ว่าย น้ำ ได้ I can swim.	*Chăn/phŏm wâai náam mâi-dâi.* ฉัน / ผม ว่าย น้ำ ไม่ได้ I can't swim.
Chăn pai tàlàat dâi-mái? ฉัน ไป ตลาด ได้ไหม Can I go to the market?	*Pai dâi.* ไป ได้ You can go.	*Pai mâi-dâi.* ไป ไม่ได้ You can't go.

Exercises

EXERCISE 4: *Listen and repeat*

1.09

Khun phôut phaa-săa à-rai? คุณ พูด ภาษา อะไร	What language do you speak?
Chăn/phŏm phôut phaa-săa-ang-krìt. ฉัน / ผม พูด ภาษาอังกฤษ	I speak English.
Khun phôut phaa-săa-thai dâi-mái. คุณ พูด ภาษาไทย ได้ไหม	Can you speak Thai?
Chăn/phŏm phôut phaa-săa-thai dâi. ฉัน / ผม พูด ภาษาไทย ได้	I can speak Thai.
Chăn/phŏm phôut phaa-săa-thai dâi nít-nòi. ฉัน / ผม พูด ภาษาไทย ได้ นิดหน่อย	I can speak a bit of Thai.
Khun săwn phaa-săa-ang-krìt dâi-mái? คุณ สอน ภาษาอังกฤษ ได้ไหม	Can you teach English?
Chăn/phŏm săwn phaa-săa-ang-krìt dâi. ฉัน / ผม สอน ภาษาอังกฤษ ได	I can teach English.
Chăn/phŏm săwn phaa-săa-ang-krìt mâi-dâi. ฉัน / ผม สอน ภาษาอังกฤษ ไม่ได้	I cannot teach English.
Khun khĭan phaa-săa-thai dâi-mái? คุณ เขียน ภาษาไทย ได้ไหม	Can you write in Thai?
Chăn/phŏm khĭan phaa-săa-thai dâi. ฉัน / ผม เขียน ภาษาไทย ได้	I can write in Thai.
Chăn/phŏm khĭan phaa-săa-thai mâi-dâi. ฉัน / ผม เขียน ภาษาไทย ไม่ได้	I cannot write in Thai.

Khun àan phaa-sǎa-sà-pen dâi-mái?	Can you read Spanish?
คุณ อ่าน ภาษาสเปน ได้ไหม	
Chǎn/phǒm àan phaa-sǎa-sà-pen dâi.	I can read Spanish.
ฉัน / ผม อ่าน ภาษาสเปน ได้	
Chǎn/phǒm àan phaa-sǎa-sà-pen mâi-dâi.	I cannot read Spanish.
ฉัน / ผม อ่าน ภาษาสเปน ไม่ได้	

EXERCISE 5: Make up questions and answers, then practice.

Q: ....

A: ....

Q: ....

A: ....

Q: ....

A: ....

Q: ....

A: ....

Cultural Notes

✪ **The *wâi***

Thais do not traditionally shake hands when they meet. They make a slight bow with the palms pressed together, called the ***wâi***. When someone gives the ***wâi*** to you, you should always return the ***wâi*** as a sign of respect. (Buddhist monks do not have to do so as they are considered representatives of the Buddha.) Younger people are expected to initiate the ***wâi*** to the elders first. The ***wâi*** is not just for greetings or paying respects, it also expresses gratitude and apology.

To perform the ***wâi***, put the palms together and raise them up. Bend the head to the hands with the tips of the index fingers between the eyebrows and the thumbs placed on the nose. There are three levels of giving ***wâi***, depending on age and social status:

- For a Buddha image or a Buddhist monk, the thumbs are at the eyebrow level.
- For parents or an elder or a person of a higher status, the thumbs are at the nose level.
- For people of the same age or social status, and for returning a ***wâi***, the thumbs are at your chest level and the forefingers touch the tip of the nose.

When it is intended as a form of greeting or farewell, people would say ***sà-wàt-dii*** while performing the ***wâi***.

✪ **Greetings and goodbyes**

Thai people normally say ***sà-wàt-dii khâ*** (women) or ***sà-wàt-dii khráp*** (men) when greeting or saying goodbye. You can say ***sà-wàt-dii*** for "hi," "good morning," "good afternoon," or "good evening."

✪ **Names and titles**

Nicknames are commonly used in Thailand. Thais may give you their nicknames instead of their first names. However, in general Thai given names are preceded by ***Khun***, unless they carry a title, such as doctor. Khun is used for men and women, married or single. For example, Malee (given name) + Sookjai (family name) is Khun Malee. If you don't know a person's name, address them as Khun.

LESSON 2

Food

In this lesson you will learn how to accept and decline food, how to order food in a restaurant, and how to count from 1 to 10.

DIALOGUE 1: *Listen and repeat*

2.01

Jim: ***Khun tham-aa-hăan à-rai khráp?***
คุณ ทำอาหาร อะไร ครับ
What are you cooking?

Chai: ***Phŏm thâwt plaa khráp. Khun Jim hĭw mái khráp?***
ผม ทอด ปลา ครับ   คุณจิม หิว ไหม ครับ
I'm deep-frying fish. Are you hungry, Jim?

Jim: ***Hĭw khráp.***
หิว ครับ
Yes, I am *(lit. I'm hungry)*.

Chai: ***Khun Jim kin plaa thâwt mái khráp?***
คุณจิม กิน ปลา ทอด ไหม ครับ
Would you like some fried fish?

Jim: ***Kin khráp. Khàwp-khun khráp.***
กิน ครับ   ขอบคุณ ครับ
Yes, please. Thank you.

(10 minutes later)

Chai: ***Khun Jim ìm mái khráp?***
คุณจิม อิ่ม ไหม ครับ
Are you full?

Jim:　　**Phǒm ìm láew khráp.**
ผม อิ่ม แล้ว ครับ
Yes, I am *(lit.* I am already full*)*.

Chai:　**Plaa thâwt à-ròi mái khráp?**
ปลาทอด อร่อย ไหม ครับ
Is the fried fish delicious?

Jim:　　**À-ròi khráp.**
อร่อย ครับ
Yes, it is. (Lit.: It's delicious)

Numbers *Listen and repeat*

0	**sǒun**	ศูนย์	4	**sìi**	สี่	8	**pàet**	แปด
1	**nùeng**	หนึ่ง	5	**hâa**	ห้า	9	**kâo**	เก้า
2	**sǎwng**	สอง	6	**hòk**	หก	10	**sìp**	สิบ
3	**sǎam**	สาม	7	**jèt**	เจ็ด			

Cooking *Listen and repeat*

tham-aa-hǎan	ทำอาหาร	cook
tôm	ต้ม	boil
thâwt	ทอด	deep-fry
phàt	ผัด	stir-fry
yâang	ย่าง	grill
nûeng	นึ่ง	steam

Food *Listen and repeat*

mŏu	หมู	pork
kài	ไก่	chicken
plaa	ปลา	fish
kûng	กุ้ง	shrimp, prawn
khài	ไข่	egg
khâaw	ข้าว	rice
khâaw-nĭaw	ข้าวเหนียว	sticky rice
sôm-tam	ส้มตำ	papaya salad
phàk	ผัก	vegetable
nám	น้ำ	water
phŏn-lá-mái	ผลไม้	fruit

Talking about food *Listen and repeat*

kin	กิน	eat
châwp	ชอบ	like
mâi-châwp	ไม่ชอบ	dislike
hĭw	หิว	hungry
mâi-hĭw	ไม่หิว	not hungry
à-ròi	อร่อย	delicious, yummy
mâi-à-ròi	ไม่อร่อย	not delicious, not yummy
ìm	อิ่ม	full

mâi-ìm	ไม่อิ่ม	not full
láew	แล้ว	already

PATTERN PRACTICE 1:

◼ What are you cooking?

Khun	*tham-aa-hǎan*	*à-rai?*
คุณ	ทำอาหาร	อะไร
You	cook	what?

◼ I am boiling eggs.

Chǎn	*tôm*	*khài.*
ฉัน	ต้ม	ไข่
I (women)	boil	eggs
Phǒm	*thâwt*	*plaa.*
ผม	ทอด	ปลา
I (men)	deep-fry	fish.

PATTERN PRACTICE 2:

◼ What do you like to eat?

Khun	*châwp*	*kin*	*à-rai?*
คุณ	ชอบ	กิน	อะไร
You	like	eat	what?

◼ I like to eat fried chicken.

Chǎn	*châwp*	*kin*	*kài-thâwt.*
ฉัน	ชอบ	กิน	ไก่ทอด
I (women)	like	eat	fried chicken.
Phǒm			*mǒu-yâang.*
ผม			หมูย่าง
I (men)			grilled pork.

PATTERN PRACTICE 3:

- Are you hungry? / Are you full?

Khun	hǐw	mái?
คุณ	หิว	ไหม
You	hungry	are.....?
	ìm	
	อิ่ม	
	full	

- I am hungry. / I am not hungry.

Chǎn	hǐw.
ฉัน	หิว
I (women)	hungry.
Phǒm	mâi-hǐw.
ผม	ไม่หิว
I (men)	not hungry.

- I am already full.

Chǎn	ìm	láew.
ฉัน	อิ่ม	แล้ว
I (women)	full	already.
Phǒm		
ผม		
I (men)		

- I am not full.

Chǎn	mâi-ìm.
ฉัน	ไม่อิ่ม
I (women)	not full.
Phǒm	
ผม	
I (men)	

PATTERN PRACTICE 4:

■ Would you like some fried chicken?

Khun	*kin*	*kài-thâwt*	*mái khá?*
คุณ	กิน	ไก่ทอด	ไหม
You	eat	fried chicken	would you like?

■ Yes, please. / No, thank you.

Kin	*khàwp-khun.*
กิน	ขอบคุณ
Eat	thank you.

Mâi-kin
ไม่ กิน
Not eat

PATTERN PRACTICE 5:

■ Is the fried chicken delicious?

Kài-thâwt	*à-ròi*	*mái?*
ไก่ทอด	อร่อย	ไหม
Fried chicken	delicious	is?

■ The fried chicken is delicious.

Kài-thâwt	*à-ròi.*
ไก่ทอด	อร่อย
Fried chicken	delicious.

	mâi-à-ròi.
	ไม่อร่อย
	not delicious.

Grammar Corner

✪ **Are/Is...? Do/Does....?**

The word *mái* can be interpreted as both a general question and an invitation or suggestion. It is placed at the end of a sentence. To answer "yes," repeat the verb or adjective. To say "no," put *mâi* before the verb or adjective.

Question: subject + verb/adjective + *mái*
Yes: subject + verb/adjective
No: subject + *mâi* (no) + verb/adjective

Example:

Questions	Yes.	No.
Khun hǐw mái? คุณ หิว ไหม Are you hungry?	*Chǎn/phǒm hǐw.* ฉัน / ผม หิว I'm hungry.	*Chǎn/phǒm mâi hǐw.* ฉัน / ผม ไม่หิว I'm not hungry.
Kâo-jai mái? เข้าใจ ไหม Do you understand?	*Kâo-jai.* เข้าใจ I understand.	*Mâi kâo-jai.* ไม่เข้าใจ I don't understand.

Exercises

EXERCISE 1: *Listen and repeat*

2.06

Khun tham-aa-hăan à-rai? คุณ ทำอาหาร อะไร	What are you cooking?
Chăn/phŏm thâwt plaa. ฉัน / ผม ทอด ปลา	I am frying fish.
Chăn/phŏm phàt mŏu. ฉัน / ผม ผัด หมู	I am cooking a pork stir-fry.
Khun châwp kin à-rai. คุณ ชอบ กิน อะไร	What do you like to eat?
Chăn/phŏm châwp kin kài-yâang. ฉัน / ผม ชอบ กิน ไก่ย่าง	I like to eat grilled chicken.
Khun hĭw mái? คุณ หิว ไหม	Are you hungry?
Chăn/phŏm hĭw. ฉัน / ผม หิว	I am hungry.
Chăn/phŏm mâi- hĭw. ฉัน / ผม ไม่หิว	I am not hungry.
Kin mŏu-yâang mái. กิน หมูย่าง ไหม	Would you like to eat grilled pork?
Kin khâ/khráp khàwp-khun khâ/khráp. กิน ค่ะ / ครับ ขอบคุณค่ะ / ครับ	Yes, please.
Mâi kin khâ/khráp khàwp-khun khâ/khráp. ไม่กิน ค่ะ / ครับ ขอบคุณค่ะ / ครับ	No, thank you.
Sôm-tam à-ròi mái? ส้มตำ อร่อย ไหม	Is the papaya salad delicious?

Sôm-tam à-ròi.
ส้มตำ อร่อย

It is delicious.

Sôm-tam mâi à-ròi .
ส้มตำ ไม่ อร่อย

It is not delicious.

2.07

EXERCISE 2: List the words from 1–16 as you hear them.

_____ pork   _____ egg   _____ rice   _____ water

_____ chicken   _____ fish   _____ vegetables   _____ fruit

_____ deep-fry   _____ grill   _____ cook   _____ steam

_____ eat   _____ hungry   _____ yummy   _____ boil

EXERCISE 3: Add words you know to complete the sentence.

1. Is the _____ delicious?

   _____ *à-ròi* _____?

2. What are you _____?

   Khun _____ *à-rai?*

3. I am _____.

   Chăn/phŏm _____.

4. Would you like _____?

   _____ *mái?*

DIALOGUE 2: *Listen and repeat*

Jim and his Thai friend Chai are ordering a meal in a restaurant.

Waiter: ***Sàng à-rai khráp?***
สั่ง อะไร ครับ
What would you like to order?

Chai: ***Khǎw sôm-tam sǎwng jaan khráp.***
ขอ ส้มตำ 2 จาน ครับ
We'd like two papaya salads, please.

Waiter: ***Sài prík mái khráp?***
ใส่ พริก ไหม ครับ
Would you like to add some chili pepper?

Jim: ***Mâi-sài khráp.***
ไม่ใส่ ครับ
No, thanks.

Chai: ***Sôm-tam pen-yang-ngai khráp?***
ส้มตำ เป็นยังไง ครับ
How is the papaya salad?

Jim: ***À-ròi kàp phèt nít-nòi khráp.***
อร่อย กับ เผ็ด นิดหน่อย ครับ
It is delicious and a bit spicy.

Ordering *Listen and repeat*

sàng	สั่ง	to order
khǎw	ขอ	I'd like . . . / May I have . . . ?
sài	ใส่	add, put
mâi-sài	ไม่ใส่	not add, without
kàp	กับ	and, with

Ingredients and taste *Listen and repeat*

prík	พริก	chili pepper
kluea	เกลือ	salt
nám-taan	น้ำตาล	sugar
nám-plaa	น้ำปลา	fish sauce
má-naaw	มะนาว	lime
phèt	เผ็ด	spicy
wǎan	หวาน	sweet
khem	เค็ม	salty
prîaw	เปรี้ยว	sour

Eating utensils *Listen and repeat*

jaan	จาน	dish, plate
cháwn	ช้อน	spoon
sâwm	ส้อม	fork
mîit	มีด	knife
kâew	แก้ว	glass

PATTERN PRACTICE 6:

■ I'd like one papaya salad, please.

Khǎw	*sôm-tam*	*nùeng*	*jaan.*
ขอ	ส้มตำ		จาน
I'd like	papaya salad	1	dish.
	kài-yâang	*sǎwng*	
	ไก่ย่าง		
	grilled chicken	2	
	khâaw-phàt	*sǎam*	
	ข้าวผัด		
	fried rice	3	

PATTERN PRACTICE 7:

■ Would you like to add some chili pepper?

Sài	*prík*	*mái?*
ใส่	พริก	ไหม
Add	chili pepper	would you like?
	nám-plaa	
	น้ำ ปลา	
	fish sauce	
	má-naaw	
	มะนาว	
	lime	

■ Yes, please. / No, thank you.

Sài khâ /khráp.
ใส่ ค่ะ / ครับ
Yes, please.

Mâi-sài khâ/khráp.
ไม่ใส่ ค่ะ / ครับ
No, thanks.

PATTERN PRACTICE 8:

■ I'd like papaya salad with sugar.

Khăw	*sôm-tam*	*sài*	*nám-taan.*
ขอ	ส้มตำ	ใส่	น้ำตาล
I'd like	papaya salad	add	sugar.
		mâi-sài	*prík*
		ไม่ใส่	พริก
		not add	chili pepper.

PATTERN PRACTICE 9:

■ How is the papaya salad?

Sôm-tam	*pen-yang-ngai?*
ส้มตำ	เป็นยังไง
Papaya salad	how is?
Kài-yâang	
ไก่ย่าง	
Grilled chicken	

■ It's sweet and delicious.

Sôm-tam	*wăan*	*kàp*	*à-ròi.*
ส้มตำ	หวาน	กับ	อร่อย
Papaya salad	sweet	and	delicious.
	phèt		
	เผ็ด		
	spicy		
	prîaw		
	ไม่เปรี้ยว		
	not sour		

Grammar Corner

✪ **How is/are . . . ?**

The phrase ***pen-yang-ngai*** is used to ask about a characteristic, state, or conditions. It is always placed at the end of a sentence.

Question : subject + verb to be (pen) + yang-ngai
Answer   : subject + adjective

Questions	Answer
Khâaw-phàt pen-yang-ngai? ข้าวผัด เป็นยังไง How is the fried rice?	***Khâaw-phàt à-ròi.*** ข้าวผัด อร่อย The fried rice is delicious.

Exercises

EXERCISE 4: *Listen and repeat*

2.12

Sàng à-rai?
สั่ง อะไร

What would you like to order?

Khǎw sôm-tam nùeng jaan.
ขอ ส้มตำ 1 จาน

I'd like one papaya salad.

Sài prík mái?
ใส่ พริก ไหม

Would you like to add some chili pepper?

Sài khâ /khráp.
ใส่ ค่ะ / ครับ

Yes, please.

Mâi-sài khâ/khráp.
ไม่ใส่ ค่ะ / ครับ

No, thanks.

Khǎw sôm-tam mâi-sài prík sǎwng jaan.
ขอ ส้มตำ ไม่ใส่ พริก 2 จาน

I'd like 2 papaya salads without chili pepper.

Sôm-tam pen-yang-ngai?
ส้มตำ เป็นยังไง

How is the papaya salad?

Sôm-tam phèt.
ส้มตำ เผ็ด

It is spicy.

Kài-yâang pen-yang-ngai?
ไก่ย่าง เป็นยังไง

How is the fried chicken?

Kài-yâang à-ròi.
ไกย่าง อร่อย

It is delicious.

Cultural Notes

✪ **Thai Food**

Thai food has become popular all around the world. It is known for its balanced combinations of at least five fundamental tastes in each dish or the overall meal; spicy, sour, sweet, salty, and bitter.

Rice is the staple food at every meal for most people. As well as rice, a traditional meal will include a soup, a curry dish with condiments, a dip with accompanying fish and vegetables, and a spicy salad. Whereas in central and southern Thailand white rice is eaten, in the north and northeast people eat sticky rice.

Thai food was traditionally eaten with the right hand while seated on mats on the floor as still happens in some households. These days, however, food is generally eaten with a fork and a spoon. All food is brought to the table at once rather than being served in courses and each dish is made to shared by everyone at the table. The more people present, the more flavors can be enjoyed!

LESSON 3
Family

In this lesson you will learn numbers from 11 upward, and how to talk about family members, age, and occupation. You will also learn how to use possessive pronouns and the verb "to have."

DIALOGUE: *Listen and repeat*

3.01

Malee: ***Krâwp-krua khǎwng-khun Jim mii kìi khon khá?***
ครอบครัว ของ คุณจิม มี กี่ คน คะ
How many people are there in your family, Jim?

Jim: ***Krâwp-krua khǎwng-phǒm mii hâa khon khráp.***
ครอบครัว ของผม มี 5 คน ครับ
There are five people in my family.

Malee: ***Mii khrai bâang khá?***
มี ใคร บ้าง คะ
Who are they?

Jim: ***Mii phâw, mâe, phîi-chaay, náwng-sǎaw kàp phǒm khráp.***
มี พ่อ แม่ พี่ชาย น้องสาว กับ ผม ครับ
They are my father, mother, older brother, younger sister, and me.

Khun Malee mii phîi-náwng kìi khon khráp?
คุณ มาลี มี พี่น้อง กี่ คน ครับ
How many siblings do you have, Malee?

Malee: ***Chǎn mii phîi-sǎaw nùeng khon kàp náwng-chaay sǎwng khon khâ.***
ฉัน มี พี่สาว หนึ่ง คน กับ น้องชาย สอง คน ค่ะ
I have one older sister and two younger brothers.

Jim: **Khun Malee aa-yú kìi pii khráp?**
คุณมาลี อายุ กี่ ปี ครับ
How old are you, Malee?

Malee: **Chăn aa-yú yîi-sìp pii khâ.**
ฉัน อายุ 20 ปี ค่ะ
I am 20 years old.

Jim: **Khun Malee tham-ngaan à-rai khráp?**
คุณมาลี ทำงาน อะไร ครับ
What do you do?

Malee: **Chăn pen nák-sùek-săa khâ.**
ฉัน เป็น นักศึกษา ค่ะ
I'm a university student.

3.02

Numbers *Listen and repeat*

11	**sìp-èt**	สิบเอ็ด		21	**yîi-sìp-èt**	ยี่สิบเอ็ด
12	**sìp-săwng**	สิบสอง		22	**yîi-sìp-săwng**	ยี่สิบสอง
13	**sìp-săam**	สิบสาม		23	**yîi-sìp-săam**	ยี่สิบสาม
14	**sìp-sìi**	สิบสี่		24	**yîi-sìp-sìi**	ยี่สิบสี่
15	**sìp-hâa**	สิบห้า		25	**yîi-sìp-hâa**	ยี่สิบห้า
16	**sìp-hòk**	สิบหก		26	**yîi-sìp-hòk**	ยี่สิบหก
17	**sìp-jèt**	สิบเจ็ด		27	**yîi-sìp-jèt**	ยี่สิบเจ็ด
18	**sìp-pàet**	สิบแปด		28	**yîi-sìp-pàet**	ยี่สิบแปด
19	**sìp-kâo**	สิบเก้า		29	**yîi-sìp-kâo**	ยี่สิบเก้า
20	**yîi-sìp**	ยี่สิบ		30	**săam-sìp**	สามสิบ

31	*săam-sìp-èt*	สามสิบเอ็ด
40	*sìi-sìp*	สี่สิบ
50	*hâa-sìp*	ห้าสิบ
60	*hòk-sìp*	หกสิบ
70	*jèt-sìp*	เจ็ดสิบ
80	*pàet-sìp*	แปดสิบ
90	*kâo-sìp*	เก้าสิบ
100	*nùeng-ráwy*	หนึ่งร้อย
101	*nùeng-ráwy-èt*	หนึ่งร้อยเอ็ด
120	*nùeng-ráwy yîi-sìp*	หนึ่งร้อย ยี่สิบ
245	*săwng-ráwy-sìi-sìp-hâa*	สองร้อย สี่สิบห้า
680	*hòk-ráwy-pàet-sìp*	หกร้อย แปดสิบ
1000	*nùeng-phan*	หนึ่งพัน

1971 **nùeng-phan-kâo-ráwy jèt-sìp-èt**
หนึ่งพัน เก้าร้อย เจ็ดสิบเอ็ด

2014 **săwng-phan-sìp-sìi**
สองพัน สิบสี่

2554 **săwng-phan-hâa-ráwy hâa-sìp-sìi**
สองพัน ห้าร้อย ห้าสิบสี่

3.03

Family members *Listen and repeat*

krâwp-krua	ครอบครัว	family
pòu	ปู่	paternal grandfather
yâa	ย่า	paternal grandmother
taa	ตา	maternal grandfather
yaay	ยาย	maternal grandmother
phâw	พ่อ	father
mâe	แม่	mother
phîi-chaay	พี่ชาย	older brother
phîi-sǎaw	พี่สาว	older sister
náwng-chaay	น้องชาย	younger brother
náwng-sǎaw	น้องสาว	younger sister
sǎa-mii	สามี	husband
phan-yaa	ภรรยา	wife
lôuk-chaay	ลูกชาย	son
lôuk-sǎow	ลูกสาว	daughter
khǎwng-khun	ของคุณ	your
khǎwng-chǎn (women) *khǎwng-phǒm* (men)	ของฉัน ของผม	my
mii	มี	have, there is/are
mâi-mii	ไม่มี	there is no....

phîi-náwng	พี่น้อง	sibling
khon	คน	person (classifier)
aa-yú	อายุ	age
pii	ปี	year
bâang	บ้าง *	else (particle)
kàp	กับ	and, with

* **Note: *Bâang*** บ้าง is placed after a question word. It is used when more than one answer to the question is possible.

Work Listen *and repeat*

3.04

aa-jaan	อาจารย์	lecturer
nák-sùek-săa	นักศึกษา	university student
nák-thú-rá-kìt	นักธุรกิจ	businessman
măw	หมอ	doctor
phá-yaa-baan	พยาบาล	nurse
tam-rùat	ตำรวจ	police officer
thá-hăan	ทหาร	soldier
tham-ngaan	ทำงาน	to work (verb), job (noun)
pen	เป็น	to be
krou	ครู	teacher
nák-rian	นักเรียน	student

3.05

Question words

kìi	กี่	How many...?
khrai	ใคร	Who..?
à-rai	อะไร	What..?

PATTERN PRACTICE 1:

■ How many people are there in your family?

Krâwp-krua	khǎwng-khun	mii	kìi	khon.
ครอบครัว	ของคุณ	มี	กี่	คน
Family	your	have	how many	person

■ There are five people in my family.

Krâwp-krua	khǎwng-chǎn	mii	hâa	khon.
ครอบครัว	ของฉัน	มี		คน
Family	my (women)	have	five	person.
	khǎwng-phǒm			
	ของผม			
	my (men)			

PATTERN PRACTICE 2:

■ Who are they?

Mii	khrai	bâang?
มี	ใคร	บ้าง*
Have	who	else?

* **Note:** The word **bâang** is placed after a question word when more than one answer to the question is possible.

■ My father, mother, older brother, younger sister, and me.

Mii	phâw, mâe, phîi-chaay, náwng-sǎaw	kàp	chǎn/phǒm.
มี	พ่อ, แม่, พี่ชาย, น้องสาว	กับ	ฉัน / ผม
They are	father, mother, older brother, younger sister,	and	me.

PATTERN PRACTICE 3:

■ How many siblings do you have?

Khun	mii	phîi-náwng	kìi	khon?
คุณ	มี	พี่น้อง	กี่	คน
You	have	siblings	how many	person (classifier)?

■ I have one older sister.

Chǎn/phǒm	mii	phîi-sǎaw	nùeng	khon.
ฉัน / ผม	มี	พี่สาว	1	คน
I	have	older sister		person (classifier).
		náwng-chaay	sǎwng	
		น้องชาย	2	
		younger brother		

■ I have no siblings.

Chǎn/phǒm	mâi-mii	phîi-náwng.
ฉัน / ผม	ไม่มี	พี่น้อง
I	have none	siblings.

PATTERN PRACTICE 4:

■ How old are you?

Khun	aa-yú	kìi	pii.
คุณ	อายุ	กี่	ปี
You	age	how many	year?
Phâw			
พ่อ			
Father			
Phîi-chaay			
พี่ชาย			
Older brother			
Náwng-sǎaw			
น้องสาว			
Younger sister			

■ I am 19 years old.

Chǎn/phǒm	aa-yú	sìp-kâo	pii.
ฉัน / ผม	อายุ	19	ปี
I	age		year.
Phâw		hâa- sìp	
พ่อ		50	
Father			
Phîi-chaay		yîi-sìp-hâa	
พี่ชาย		25	
Older brother			
Náwng-sǎaw		sìp-pàet	
น้องสาว		18	
Younger sister			

PATTERN PRACTICE 5:

■ What do you do?

Khun	*tham-ngaan*	*à-rai?*
คุณ	ทำงาน	อะไร
you	job	what?

Phâw
พ่อ
Father

Phîi-chaay
พี่ชาย
Older brother

Náwng- sǎaw
น้องสาว
Younger sister

■ I am a university student.

Chǎn/phǒm	*pen*	*nák-sùek-sǎa.*
ฉัน / ผม	เป็น	นักศึกษา
I	to be	university student.

Phâw		*nák-thú-rá-kìt*
พ่อ		นักธุรกิจ
Father		businessman.

Phîi-chaay		*thá-hǎan.*
พี่ชาย		ทหาร
Older brother		soldier.

Náwng-sǎaw		*nák-rian.*
น้องสาว		นักเรียน
Younger sister		student.

Grammar Corner

✪ **Possessive adjectives**

Possessive adjectives are always placed after the noun.

Personal pronouns	Possessive adjectives
chǎn/phǒm ฉัน / ผม I	*khǎwng-chǎn/khǎwng-phǒm* ของฉัน / ของผม my
khun คุณ you	*khǎwng-khun* ของคุณ your
khǎo เขา he/she/they	*khǎwng-khǎo* ของเขา his/her/their
rao เรา we	*khǎwng-rao* ของเรา our

Example:

*Krâwp-krua **khǎwng-chǎn** mii sìi khon.*
ครอบครัว ของฉัน มี 4 คน

There are four people in my family.

*Phâw **khǎwng-khun** tham-ngaan à-rai?*
พ่อ ของคุณ ทำงาน อะไร

What is your father's job?

❷ **How many?**

The word *kìi* is placed before the classifier for the object.

Subject + verb + object (noun) + ***kìi*** (How many?) + classifier

Example:

Khun mii phîi-náwng __kìi__ khon?

คุณ มี พี่น้อง กี่ คน

How many siblings do you have?

Khun aa-yú __kìi__ pii?

คุณ อายุ กี่ ปี

How old are you?

Exercises

EXERCISE 1: *Listen and repeat*

3.06

Khun chûe à-rai?

คุณ ชื่อ อะไร

What's your name?

Phǒm chûe Jim khráp./Chǎn chûe Malee khâ.

ผม ชื่อ จิม ครับ / ฉัน ชื่อ มาลี ค่ะ

My name is Jim/Malee.

Krâwp-krua khǎwng-khun mii kìi khon?

ครอบครัว ของคุณ มี กี่ คน

How many people are there in your family?

Krâwp-krua khǎwng-chǎn/khǎwng-phǒm mii sìi khon.

ครอบครัว ของฉัน / ของผม มี 4 คน

There are four people in my family.

Mii khrai bâang?

มี ใคร บ้าง

Who are they?

Mii phâw, mâe, phîi-sǎaw, kàp chǎn/phǒm.

มี พ่อ แม่ พี่สาว กับ ฉัน / ผม

They are my father, mother, older sister, and me.

Khun mii phîi-náwng kìi khon?

คุณ มี พี่น้อง กี่ คน

How many siblings do you have?

Chǎn/phǒm mii phîi-sǎaw nùeng khon kàp náwng-chaay nùeng khon.

ฉัน / ผม มี พี่สาว 1 คน กับน้องชาย 1 คน

I have one older sister and one younger brother.

Chǎn/phǒm mâi-mii phîi-náwng. ฉัน / ผม ไม่มี พี่น้อง	I have no brothers or sisters.
Khun aa-yú kìi pii. คุณ อายุ กี่ ปี	How old are you?
Chǎn/phǒm aa-yú yîi-sìp pii. ฉัน / ผม อายุ 20 ปี	I am 20 years old.
Náwng-chaay aa-yú kìi pii. น้องชาย อายุ กี่ ปี	How old is your younger brother?
Náwng-chaay aa-yú sìp-hâa pii. น้องชาย อายุ 15 ปี	He is 15 years old.
Phîi-sǎaw chûe à-rai? พี่สาว ชื่อ อะไร	What is your older sister's name?
Phâw tham-ngaan à-rai? พ่อ ทำงาน อะไร	What is your father's job?
Phâw pen nák-thú-rá-kìt. พ่อ เป็น นักธุรกิจ	He is a businessman.

EXERCISE 2: Ask and answer these questions in Thai.

1. How many people are there in your family?
2. Who are they?
3. How many brothers/sisters do you have?
4. What is your brother/sister's name?
5. How old are you?
6. How old is your brother/sister?
7. What is your father's job?
8. What is your mother's job?

EXERCISE 3: Translation practice.

Translate the description of Ann's family into Thai. Use the language on pages 53–54 to help you.

My name is Ann. I have 3 siblings. I have an older brother and one younger brother. I am 19 years old. My brothers are 25 and 16 years old. My father is a police officer. My mother is a nurse.

Cultural Notes

✪ The Thai family

The Thai family is a form of hierarchy with the parents at the top. Families are often extended, with parents, children, grandparents, aunts and cousins all living together in the same house. Children are taught to honor their parents. In Thailand, most parents work, especially in urban households. It is very rare that a mother remains at home as a housewife.

LESSON 4

What time is it?

In this lesson you will learn how to tell the time and how to talk about everyday activities and daily routines using time expressions.

DIALOGUE: *Listen and repeat*

Aarii: ***Khun Jim tùen-nawn kìi-mong khá?***
คุณจิม ตื่นนอน กี่โมง คะ
What time do you get up, Jim?

Jim: ***Phǒm tùen-nawn hòk-mong-cháo khráp.***
ผม ตื่นนอน 6 โมงเช้า ครับ
I get up at 6 a.m.

Aarii: ***Khun Jim pai rong-rian kìi-mong khá?***
คุณจิม ไป โรงเรียน กี่โมง คะ
What time do you go to school?

Jim: ***Phǒm pai rong-rian kâo-mong-cháo khráp.***
ผม ไป โรงเรียน 9 โมงเช้า ครับ
I go to school at 9 a.m.

Aarii: ***Tawn-bàay Khun Jim tham-à-rai khá?***
ตอนบ่าย คุณจิม ทำ อะไร คะ
What do you do in the afternoon?

Jim: ***Tawn-bàay phǒm tham-kaan-bâan láew-kâw àan-nǔng-sǔe khráp.***
ตอนบ่าย ผม ทำการบ้าน แล้วก็ อ่านหนังสือ ครับ
In the afternoon, I do my homework, then read a book.

> *Krou Aarii klàp bâan kìi-mong khráp?*
> ครูอารี กลับ บ้าน กี่โมง ครับ
> What time do you go home, Teacher Aarii?

Aarii: *Chăn klàp bâan săam-thûm khâ.*
ฉัน กลับ บ้าน 3 ทุ่ม ค่ะ
I go home at 9 p.m.

Telling the time *Listen and repeat*

4.02

tii	ตี ...	morning 1 a.m. – 5 a.m.
mong-cháo	... โมงเช้า	morning 6 a.m. – 11 a.m.
thîang-wan	เที่ยงวัน	noon
bàay ... mong	บ่าย ... โมง	afternoon from 1 p.m. – 3 p.m.
mong-yen	... โมงเย็น	evening from 4 p.m. – 6 p.m.
thûm	... ทุ่ม	night from 7 p.m. – 11 p.m.
thîang-khuen	เที่ยงคืน	midnight
krûeng	... ครึ่ง	half
naa-thii	... นาที	minute

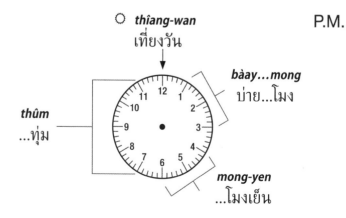

Times of day *Listen and repeat*

A.M.

thîang-khuen	เที่ยงคืน	midnight
tii-nùeng	ตี 1	1 a.m.
tii-sǎwng	ตี 2	2 a.m.
tii-sǎam	ตี 3	3 a.m.
tii-sìi	ตี 4	4 a.m.
tii-hâa	ตี 5	5 a.m.
hòk-mong-cháo	6 โมงเช้า	6 a.m.
jèt-mong-cháo	7 โมงเช้า	7 a.m.
pàet-mong-cháo	8 โมงเช้า	8 a.m.
kâo-mong-cháo	9 โมงเช้า	9 a.m.
sìp-mong-cháo	10 โมงเช้า	10 a.m.
sìp-èt-mong-cháo	11 โมงเช้า	11 a.m.

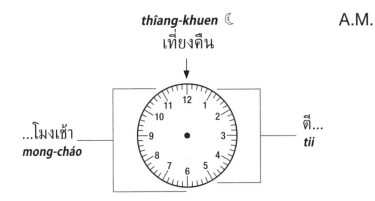

thîang-khuen ☾   **A.M.**
เที่ยงคืน

...โมงเช้า   ตี...
mong-cháo   *tii*

P.M.

thîang (wan)	เที่ยง (วัน)	noon
bàay-(nùeng)-mong	บ่าย (1) โมง	1 p.m.

*Note: 1 p.m. can be said either *bàay-nùeng-mong* or just *bàay-mong* without using the number one.

bàay-sǎwng-mong	บ่าย 2 โมง	2 p.m.
bàay-sǎam-mong	บ่าย 3 โมง	3 p.m.
sìi-mong-yen	4 โมงเย็น	4 p.m.
hâa-mong-yen	5 โมงเย็น	5 p.m.
hòk-mong-yen	6 โมงเย็น	6 p.m.
nùeng-thûm	1 ทุ่ม	7 p.m.
sǎwng-thûm	2 ทุ่ม	8 p.m.
sǎam-thûm	3 ทุ่ม	9 p.m.
sìi-thûm	4 ทุ่ม	10 p.m.
hâa-thûm	5 ทุ่ม	11 p.m.

PATTERN PRACTICE 1:

■ What time is it?

Kìi-mong?
กี่โมง
What time is it? (day time)

Kìi-thûm?
กี่ทุ่ม
What time is it? (night time)

PATTERN PRACTICE 2:

■ Clock Times

4 a.m.	=	*tii-sìi* ตี 4
5:05 a.m.	=	*tii-hâa-hâa-naa-thii* ตี 5 5 นาที
8:10 a.m.	=	*pàet-mong-cháo-sìp-naa-thii* 8 โมงเช้า10 นาที
11:15 a.m.	=	*sìp-èt-mong-cháo-sìp-hâa-naa-thii* 11 โมงเช้า15 นาที
12:20 p.m.	=	*thîang(wan)-yîi-sìp-naa-thii* เที่ยง (วัน) 20 นาที
1:25 p.m.	=	*bàay-(nùeng)-mong-yîi-sìp-hâa-naa-thii* บ่าย (1) โมง 25 นาที
3:30 p.m.	=	*bàay-sǎam-mong-krûeng* บ่าย 3 โมง ครึ่ง
5:35 p.m.	=	*hâa-mong-yen-sǎam-sìp-hâa-naa-thii* 5 โมงเย็น 35 นาที
6:40 p.m.	=	*hòk-mong-yen-sìi-sìp-naa-thii* 6 โมงเย็น 40 นาที
7:45 p.m.	=	*nùeng-thûm-sìi-sìp-hâa-naa-thii* 1 ทุ่ม 45 นาที
9:50 p.m.	=	*sǎam-thûm-hâa-sìp-naa-thii* 3 ทุ่ม 50 นาที
11:55 p.m.	=	*hâa-thûm-hâa-sìp-hâa-naa-thii* 5 ทุ่ม 55 นาที

Exercises

EXERCISE 1: Look at these clocks and write the time.

p.m. _____

p.m. _____

p.m. _____

a.m. _____

p.m. _____

a.m. _____

p.m. _____

midnight _____

p.m. _____

a.m. _____

p.m. _____

a.m. _____

4.04

EXERCISE 2: Listen and write the time you hear.

1. _____

2. _____

3. _____

4. _____

5. _____

6. _____

7. _____

8. _____

4.05

Daily routines *Listen and repeat*

tùen-nawn	ตื่นนอน	wake up/get up
praeng-fun	แปรงฟัน	brush teeth
láang-nâa	ล้างหน้า	wash face
àap-nám	อาบน้ำ	take a shower
sà-phŏm	สระผม	wash hair
kin-khâaw-cháo	กินข้าวเช้า	have breakfast

láang-jaan	ล้างจาน	wash dishes	
kwàat-bâan	กวาดบ้าน	sweep the room	
dou-thii-wii	ดูทีวี	watch TV	
àan-nǔng-sǔe	อ่านหนังสือ	read a book	
rôem-rian	เริ่มเรียน	start class	
lôek-rian	เลิกเรียน	finish class	
tham-kaan-bâan	ทำการบ้าน	do homework	
prà-chum	ประชุม	have a meeting	
nawn	นอน	go to bed	
láew-kâw	แล้วก็	then	
tham	ทำ	do, make	
tham-ngaan	ทำงาน	to work	
pai	ไป	go	
klàp	กลับ	get back, return	
rong-rian	โรงเรียน	school	
bâan	บ้าน	house, home	

PATTERN PRACTICE 3:

■ What time do you get up?

Khun	tùen-nawn	kìi-mong?
คุณ	ตื่นนอน	กี่โมง
You	wake up/get up	what time? (day time)
	nawn	kìi-thûm?
	นอน	กี่ทุ่ม
	go to bed	what time? (night time)

■ I get up at 7 a.m.

Chǎn/phǒm	tùen-nawn	jèt-mong-cháo.
ฉัน / ผม	ตื่นนอน	7 โมงเช้า
I	wake up/get up	7 a.m.
	nawn	sìi-thûm.
	นอน	4 ทุ่ม
	go to bed	10 p.m.

PATTERN PRACTICE 4:

■ What time do you go to school?

Khun	pai	rong-rian	kìi-mong?
คุณ	ไป	โรงเรียน	กี่โมง
You	go	school	what time? (day time)
	klàp	bâan	
	กลับ	บ้าน	
	get back	home	

- I go to school at 8 a.m.

Chăn/phŏm	pai	rong-rian	pàet-mong-cháo.
ฉัน / ผม	ไป	โรงเรียน	8 โมงเช้า
I	go	school	8 a.m.
	klàp	bâan	hòk-mong-yen.
	กลับ	บ้าน	6 โมงเย็น
	get back	home	6 p.m.

PATTERN PRACTICE 5:

- What time do you start/finish class?

Khun	rôem-rian	kìi-mong?
คุณ	เริ่มเรียน	กี่โมง
You	start class	what time? (day time)
	lôek-rian	
	เลิกเรียน	
	finish class	

- I start/finish class at . . .

Chăn/phŏm	rôem-rian	kâo-mong-cháo.
ฉัน / ผม	เริ่มเรียน	9 โมงเช้า
I	start class	9 a.m.
	lôek-rian	sìi-mong-yen.
	เลิกเรียน	4 โมงเย็น
	finish class	4 p.m.

Times of the day *Listen and repeat*

tawn-cháo	ตอนเช้า	in the morning
tawn-bàay	ตอนบ่าย	in the afternoon
tawn-yen	ตอนเย็น	in the evening
tawn-kâm	ตอนค่ำ	at night
...tham-à-rai?	...ทำ อะไร	What do/does ... do?

PATTERN PRACTICE 6:

■ What do you do in the morning?

Tawn-cháo	*khun*	*tham*	*à-rai?*
ตอนเช้า	คุณ	ทำ	อะไร
In the morning	you	do	what?
Tawn-bàay			
ตอนบ่าย			
In the afternoon			

■ I wash my face in the morning.

ตอนเช้า	ฉัน / ผม	ล้างหน้า
Tawn-cháo	*chǎn/phǒm*	*láang-nâa.*
In the morning	I	wash face.
ตอนบ่าย		กวาดบ้าน
Tawn-bàay		*kwàat-bâan.*
In the afternoon		sweep the room.

■ In the morning, I wash my face, then brush my teeth.

Tawn-cháo	*chǎn/ phǒm*	*láang-nâa*	*láew-kâw*	*praeng-fun.*
ตอนเช้า	ฉัน / ผม	ล้างหน้า	แล้วก็	แปรงฟัน
In the morning	I	wash face	then	brush teeth.
Tawn-bàay		*láang-jaan*		*doo-thii-wii.*
ตอนบ่าย		ล้างจาน		ดูทีวี
In the afternoon		wash dishes		watch TV.
Tawn-kâm		*tham-kaan-bâan*		*nawn.*
ตอนค่ำ		ทำการบ้าน		นอน
At night		do my homework		go to bed.

Grammar Corner

✪ **Linking actions**

The phrase *láew-kâw*, meaning "then," links two actions, and is placed before the verb of the second clause.

Example:

Chǎn/phǒm àap-nám láew-kâw tham-kaan-bâan.

ฉัน / ผม อาบน้ำ แล้วก็ ทำการบ้าน

I take a bath, and then do homework.

Chǎn/phǒm pai tham-ngaan láew-kâw klàp bâan.

ฉัน / ผม ไปทำงาน แล้วก็ กลับ บ้าน

I go to work, and then return home.

Exercises

4.07

EXERCISE 3: *Listen and repeat*

Khun tùen-nawn kìi-mong?

คุณ ตื่นนอน กี่โมง

What time do you get up?

Chǎn/phǒm tùen-nawn jèt-mong-cháo.

ฉัน / ผม ตื่นนอน 7 โมงเช้า

I get up at 7 a.m.

Khun nawn kìi-thûm?

คุณ นอน กี่ทุ่ม

What time do you go to bed?

Chǎn/phǒm nawn hâa thûm.

ฉัน / ผม นอน 5 ทุ่ม

I go to bed at 11 p.m.

Khun pai rong-rian kìi-mong?

คุณ ไป โรงเรียน กี่โมง

What time do you go to school?

Chǎn/phǒm pai rong-rian pàet-mong-cháo.
ฉัน / ผม ไป โรงเรียน 8 โมงเช้า

I go to school at 8 a.m.

Khun klàp bâan kìi-mong?
คุณ กลับ บ้าน กี่โมง

What time do you get home?

Chǎn/phǒm klàp bâan hòk-mong-yen.
ฉัน / ผม กลับ บ้าน 6 โมงเย็น

I get home at 6 p.m.

Khun rôem-rian kìi-mong?
คุณ เริ่มเรียน กี่โมง

What time do you start class?

Chǎn/phǒm rôem-rian kâo-mong-cháo.
ฉัน / ผม เริ่มเรียน 9 โมงเช้า

I start class at 9 am.

Khun lôek-rian kìi-mong?
คุณ เลิกเรียน กี่โมง

What time do you finish class?

Chǎn/phǒm lôek-rian sìi-mong-yen.
ฉัน / ผม เลิกเรียน 4 โมงเย็น

I finish class at 4 p.m.

Tawn-cháo khun tham-à-rai?
ตอน เช้า คุณ ทำ อะไร

What do you do in the morning?

Tawn-cháo chǎn/phǒm àap-nám.
ตอน เช้า ฉัน / ผม อาบน้ำ

I take a bath in the morning.

Tawn-kâm khun tham-à-rai?
ตอน ค่ำ คุณ ทำ อะไร

What do you do at night?

Tawn-kâm chǎn/phǒm tham-kaan-bâan
láew-kâw doo-thii-wii.
ตอน ค่ำ ฉัน / ผม ทำการบ้าน
แล้วก็ ดูทีวี

I do homework, and then watch TV.

EXERCISE 4: Question and answer practice.

Make up and practice questions and answers about the pictures using the structure "What time . . . ?"

Cultural Notes

❂ **Telling the time in Thai**

Thais use the 24 hour military time system for official announcements, but in everyday life a different and uniquely Thai system is used in which the clock is divided into 4 blocks of 5 or 6 hours, and each of these blocks of time is referred to in a different way.

tii ตี ...	early morning from 1 a.m. – 5 a.m.
mong-cháo ... โมงเช้า	morning from 6 a.m. – 11 a.m.
bàay ... mong/mong-yen บ่าย ...โมง / ... โมงเย็น	afternoon to early evening from 1 p.m. – 6 p.m.
thûm ... ทุ่ม	late evening from 7 p.m. – 11 p.m. ***Note:** when referring to 7–11 p.m., the numbers 1 – 5 are used instead of the numbers 7 – 11 and followed by the word *thûm*.

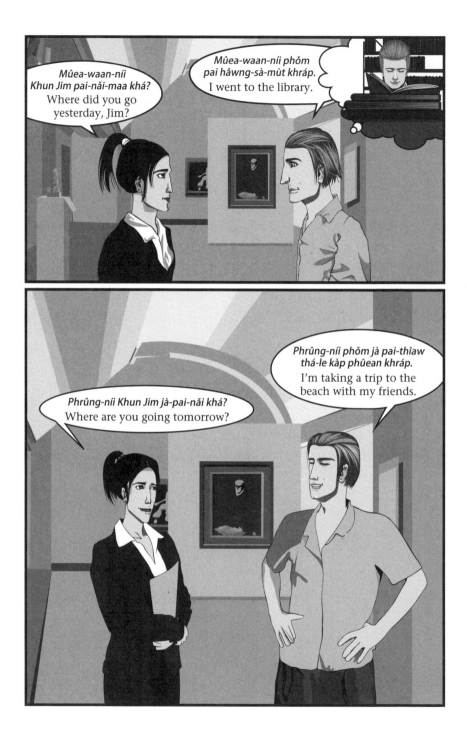

LESSON 5

Yesterday and tomorrow

In this lesson you will learn how to talk about present, past, and future events, and how to ask and answer questions about leisure activities.

DIALOGUE: *Listen and repeat*

5.01

Teacher: ***Mûea-waan-níi Khun Jim pai-nǎi-maa khá?***
เมื่อวานนี้ คุณจิม ไปไหนมา คะ
Where did you go yesterday, Jim?

Jim: ***Mûea-waan-níi phǒm pai hâwng-sà-mùt khráp.***
เมื่อวานนี้ ผม ไป ห้องสมุด ครับ
I went to the library.

Teacher: ***Phrûng-níi Khun Jim jà-pai-nǎi khá?***
พรุ่งนี้ คุณจิม จะ ไปไหน คะ
Where are you going tomorrow?

Jim: ***Phrûng-níi phǒm jà pai-thîaw thá-le kàp phûean khráp.***
พรุ่งนี้ ผม จะ ไปเที่ยว ทะเล กับ เพื่อน ครับ
I'm taking a trip to the beach with my friends.

Teacher: ***We-laa-wâang Khun Jim châwp tham-à-rai khá?***
เวลาว่าง คุณจิม ชอบ ทำ อะไร คะ
What do you like to do in your free time?

Jim: ***Phǒm châwp lên-don-trii láew-kâw ráwng-phleng khráp.***
ผม ชอบ เล่นดนตรี แล้วก็ ร้องเพลง ครับ
I like playing musical instruments and also singing.

Days of the week *Listen and repeat*

5.02

wan-jan	วันจันทร์	Monday
wang-ang-khaan	วันอังคาร	Tuesday
wan-phút	วันพุธ	Wednesday
*wan-phá-rúe-hàt	วันพฤหัส	Thursday
wan-sùk	วันศุกร์	Friday
wan-săo	วันเสาร์	Saturday
wan-aa-thít	วันอาทิตย์	Sunday

*The full word for Thursday is ***wan-phá-rúe-hàt-sà-baw-dii*** but due to its length, the abbreviated version above is usually used.

Present, past, and future *Listen and repeat*

5.03

wan	วัน	day
wan-níi	วันนี้	today
mûea-waan-níi	เมื่อวานนี้	yesterday
phrûng-níi	พรุ่งนี้	tomorrow
ìik . . . wan	อีก . . . วัน	in . . . day(s) from now
aa-thít	อาทิตย์	week
aa-thít-níi	อาทิตย์นี้	this week
aa-thít-thîi-láew	อาทิตย์ที่แล้ว	last week
aa-thít-nâa	อาทิตย์หน้า	next week
ìik . . . aa-thít	อีก . . . อาทิตย์	in . . . week(s) from now

duean	เดือน	month
duean-níi	เดือนนี้	this month
duean-thîi-láew	เดือนที่แล้ว	last month
duean-nâa	เดือนหน้า	next month
iik...duean	อีก...เดือน	in.... month(s) from now

pii	ปี	year
pii-níi	ปีนี้	this year
pii-thîi-láew	ปีที่แล้ว	last year
pii-nâa	ปีหน้า	next year
iik...pii	อีก...ปี	in.... year(s) from now

Places *Listen and repeat*

5.04

wát	วัด	temple
naa	นา	rice field
tà-làat	ตลาด	market
hâwng-sà-mùt	ห้องสมุด	library
mâe-nám	แม่น้ำ	river
nám-tòk	น้ำตก	waterfall
thá-le	ทะเล	beach, sea
phou-khǎo	ภูเขา	mountain

5.05

Leisure activities *Listen and repeat*

pai	ไป	go
tham	ทำ	do
wing	วิ่ง	run
doo-năng	ดูหนัง	see a movie
fang-phleng	ฟังเพลง	listen to music
ráwng-phleng	ร้องเพลง	sing
tên	เต้น	dance
lên-don-trii	เล่นดนตรี	play musical instruments
wâay-nám	ว่ายน้ำ	swim
khìi-jàk-kà-yaan	ขี่จักรยาน	ride a bike
doen-pàa	เดินป่า	hike
tham-sŭan	ทำสวน	gardening
pai-thîaw	ไปเที่ยว	take a trip, visit a place
we-laa-wâang	เวลาว่าง	free time
châwp	ชอบ	to like
phûean	เพื่อน	friend
kàp	กับ	and, with
láew-kâw	แล้วก็	then, also
jà	จะ	will

5.06

CONVERSATION QUESTIONS:

... pai-năi-maa? *	...ไปไหนมา	Where have ... been? Where did ... go?
... jà-pai-năi?	...จะ ไปไหน	Where will ... go?
... tham-à-rai?	...ทำ อะไร	What do/did ... do?

*Note: The ending *năi-maa*, meaning "where" is only used with the verb *pai*, "to go."

PATTERN PRACTICE 1:

■ Where did you go yesterday?

Mûea-waan-níi	*khun*	*pai-năi-maa?*
เมื่อวานนี้	คุณ	ไปไหนมา
Yesterday	you	go where?
Aa-thít-thîi-láew		*doo-năng à-rai?*
อาทิตย์ที่แล้ว		ดูหนัง อะไร
Last week		see movie what?

■ I went to the market.

Mûea-waan-níi	*chăn/phŏm*	*pai*	*tà-làat.*
เมื่อวานนี้	ฉัน / ผม	ไป	ตลาด
Yesterday	I	go	market.
Aa-thít-thîi-láew		*doo-năng*	
อาทิตย์ที่แล้ว		ดูหนังอะไร	
Last week		see	The Hunger Games.

PATTERN PRACTICE 2:

- What are you doing tomorrow?

Phrûng-níi	khun	jà	tham-à-rai?
พรุ่งนี้	คุณ	จะ	ทำ อะไร
Tomorrow	you	will	what do?
Duean-nâa			**pai-nǎi?**
เดือนหน้า			ไปไหน
Next month			where go?

- I'm going hiking with friends.

Phrûng-níi	chǎn/ phǒm	jà	pai	doen-pàa	kàp	phûean.
พรุ่งนี้	ฉัน/ผม	จะ	ไป	เดินป่า	กับ	เพื่อน
Tomorrow	I	will	go	hiking	with	a friend.
Duean-nâa			**pai-thîaw**	**thá-le**		
เดือนหน้า			ไปเที่ยว	ทะเล		
Next month			take a trip	beach		

PATTERN PRACTICE 3:

- What do you like to do in your free time?

We-laa-wâang	khun	châwp	tham-à-rai?
เวลาว่าง	คุณ	ชอบ	ทำ อะไร
Free time	you	like	What do?

- I like to listen to music.

Chǎn/phǒm	châwp	fang-phleng.
ฉัน / ผม	ชอบ	ฟังเพลง
I	like	listen to music.
		wâay-nám.
		ว่ายน้ำ
		swim.

Grammar Corner

✪ **Past, present, and future tenses**

The form of the verb does not change in Thai whether you are talking about the past or the present. The tense is implied from the context of the conversation. When talking about the future the word *jà* can be placed in front of the verb, but this is not necessary.

Chǎn/phǒm pai wát.	I go to the temple.
Chǎn/phǒm pai wát.	I went to the temple.
Chǎn/phǒm (jà) pai wát.	I'll go to the temple.

5.07

Exercises

EXERCISE 1: *Listen and repeat*

Wan-níi khun pai-nǎi-maa?
วันนี้ คุณ ไปไหนมา

Where did you go today?

Wan-níi chǎn/phǒm pai wát.
วันนี้ ฉัน / ผม ไป วัด

Today I went to the temple.

Mûea-waan-níi khun pai-nǎi-maa?
เมื่อวานนี้ คุณ ไปไหนมา

Where did you go yesterday?

Mûea-waan-níi chǎn/phǒm pai tà-làat kàp phûean.
เมื่อวานนี้ ฉัน / ผม ไป ตลาด กับ เพื่อน

Yesterday I went to the market with a friend.

Aa-thít-thîi-láew khun tham-à-rai?
อาทิตย์ที่แล้ว คุณ ทำ อะไร

What did you do last week?

Aa-thít-thîi-láew chǎn/phǒm pai doen-pàa.
อาทิตย์ที่แล้ว ฉัน / ผม ไป เดินป่า

Last week I went hiking.

Wan-níi khun jà-pai-nǎi?
วันนี้ คุณ จะ ไปไหน

Where are you going today?

Wan-níi chǎn/phǒm jà-pai hâwng-sà-mùt.
วันนี้ ฉัน / ผม จะ ไป ห้องสมุด

Today I'm going to the library.

Phrûng-níi khun jà-pai-nǎi?
พรุ่งนี้ คุณ จะไปไหน

Where are you going tomorrow?

Phrûng-níi chǎn/phǒm jà pai-thîaw thá-le kàp krâwp-krua.
พรุ่งนี้ ฉัน / ผม จะ ไปเที่ยว ทะเล กับ ครอบครัว

I'm going to the beach with my family tomorrow.

Duean-nâa khun jà tham-à-rai?
เดือนหน้า คุณ จะ ทำ อะไร

What are you doing next month?

Duean-nâa chǎn/phǒm jà klàp à-me-rí-kaa.
เดือนหน้า ฉัน / ผม จะ กลับ อเมริกา

I'm returning to America next month.

We-laa-wâang khun châwp tham-à-rai?
เวลาว่าง คุณ ชอบ ทำ อะไร

What do you like to do in your free time?

Chǎn/phǒm châwp khìi-jàk-kà-yaan.
ฉัน / ผม ชอบ ขี่จักรยาน

I like to ride my bike.

Chǎn/phǒm châwp wâay-nám.
ฉัน / ผม ชอบ ว่ายน้ำ

I like to swim.

Note: **Wan-níi (today) can be used with both questions **pai-nǎi-maa** (Where did you go?) and **jà-pai-nǎi** (Where will you go?).*

EXERCISE 2: Question and answer practice.

Make up questions and answers using the following words, then practice.

1. Next week   2. This month   3. Last year   4. Free time

EXERCISE 3: Talk about your regular activities.

Practice describing your weekly routines, using the pattern below.

1. On Monday I . . .
2. On Thursday I . . .
3. On Saturday I . . .

Cultural Notes

✪ **Popular Thai pastimes**

According to the National Statistical Office, one of the most popular leisure activities for Thai people is watching television, especially soap operas and live soccer matches. Statistics also reveal that Thais like to play games on their computers, smartphones, or tablets as well as browsing the Internet. Going to the cinema is another popular pastime and the cinemas show both Thai-made and foreign films, the latter often with subtitles.

Many Thai people also enjoy domestic travel. In Thailand, you can find over 100 national parks with spectacular mountain scenery, outstanding beaches and stunning waterfalls, and important museums and historical sites.

✪ **Where have you been?**

The questions "Where are you going?" *(jà-pai-nǎi)* or "Where have you been?" *(pai-nǎi-maa)*, can at first shock foreigners who are used to protecting their personal privacy. But they are not so much questions as a kind of greeting that does not demand a detailed explanation. A straightforward answer is not always expected; you can just say *pai-thú-rá* which means "running an errand." This is a neutral answer when you don't want to be specific.

LESSON 6
Shopping

In this lesson you will learn the language you need for shopping
and bargaining, including vocabulary for clothes, colors, and sizes.

DIALOGUE: *Listen and repeat*

6.01

Shop assistant: ***Súe à-rai khráp?***
ซื้อ อะไร ครับ
Yes, please?

Jim: ***Mii sûea sĭi daeng mái khráp?***
มี เสื้อ สีแดง ไหม ครับ
Do you have a red shirt?

Shop assistant: ***Mii khráp.***
มี ครับ
Yes, I do.

Jim: ***Lawng dâi-mái khráp?***
ลอง ได้ไหม ครับ
Can I try it on?

Shop assistant: ***Dâi khráp.***
ได้ ครับ
Yes, you can.

Jim: ***Thôa-rài khráp?***
เท่าไร ครับ
How much is it?

Shop assistant: ***Săwng-róy bàat khráp.***
200 บาท ครับ
200 baht.

Jim: ***Lót dâi-mái khráp?***
ลด ได้ไหม ครับ
Can you lower the price?

Shop assistant: ***Lót dâi yîi-sìp bàat khráp.***
ลด ได้ 20 บาท ครับ
I can offer 20 baht discount.

Shopping *Listen and repeat*

súe	ซื้อ	buy
lék	เล็ก	small
yài	ใหญ่	large
mii	มี	have
mâi-mii	ไม่มี	not have
lawng	ลอง	try on
lót	ลด	discount

QUESTION WORDS: *Listen and repeat*

thôa-rài	เท่าไร	How many/how much?
à-rai	อะไร	What...?
dâi-mái	ได้ไหม	Can ...?
mái	ไหม	Do you...?

Clothing *Listen and repeat*

	Items		*classifier*	
sûea	เสื้อ	shirt	**tua**	ตัว
kaang-keng	กางเกง	pants	**tua**	ตัว
krà-prong	กระโปรง	skirt	**tua**	ตัว
krà-pǎo	กระเป๋า	purse, bag	**bai**	ใบ
rawng-tháo	รองเท้า	shoes	**khôu**	คู่
thǔng-tháo	ถุงเท้า	socks	**khôu**	คู่

Stationery supplies *Listen and repeat*

	Items		classifier	
pàak-kaa	ปากกา	pen	**dâam**	ด้าม
din-sǎw	ดินสอ	pencil	**thâeng**	แท่ง
nǎng-sǔe	หนังสือ	book	**lêm**	เล่ม
sà-mùt	สมุด	notebook	**lêm**	เล่ม

Toiletries *Listen and repeat*

	Items		classifier	
sà-bòu	สบู่	soap	**kâwn**	ก้อน
praeng-sǐi-fan	แปรงสีฟัน	toothbrush	**an**	อัน
yaa-sǐi-fan	ยาสีฟัน	toothpaste	**làwt**	หลอด
yaa-sà-phǒm	ยาสระผม	shampoo	**khùat**	ขวด

PATTERN PRACTICE 1:

■ Yes, please? (*Lit:* What would you like to buy?)

Súe	*à-rai?*
ซื้อ	อะไร
Buy	what?

■ I'd like (to buy) . . .

Súe	*yaa-sà-phŏm*	*nùeng*	*khùat.*
ซื้อ	ยาสระผม	1	ขวด
Buy	shampoo		
	prang-sĭi-fan	*săwng*	*an.*
	แปรงสีฟัน	2	อัน
	toothbrush		
	sûea	*săam*	*tua.*
	เสื้อ	3	ตัว
	shirt		
	rawng-tháo	*sìi*	*khôu.*
	รองเท้า	4	คู่
	pair of shoes		
	pàak-kaa	*hăa*	*dâam.*
	ปากกา	5	ด้าม
	pen		
	din-săw	*hòk*	*thâeng.*
	ดินสอ	6	แท่ง
	pencil		

Grammar Corner

✪ **Classifiers**

Classifiers are used when you want to count objects. Each object has a specific classifier word that should be used when you are stating the quantity of that object.

noun + number/quantity + classifier		
sûea săwng tua	เสื้อ 2 ตัว	two shirts
năng-sŭe săam lêm	หนังสือ 3 เล่ม	three books

Color *Listen and repeat*

sĭi	สี	color
dam	ดำ	black
daeng	แดง	red
khăaw	ขาว	white
nám-ngoen	น้ำเงิน	navy blue
fáa	ฟ้า	blue
lŭeang	เหลือง	yellow
sôm	ส้ม	orange
khĭaw	เขียว	green
chom-phou	ชมพู	pink
mûang	ม่วง	purple
nám-taan	น้ำตาล	brown

PATTERN PRACTICE 2:

■ Do you have a black shirt?

Mii	*sûea*	*sǐi*	*dam*	*mái?*
มี	เสื้อ	สี	ดำ	ไหม
Have	shirt	color	black	do you...?
	kaang-keng	*khôu*	*nám-ngoen*	
	กางเกง	คู่	น้ำเงิน	
	pants	pair	navy blue	
	rawng-tháo		*yài*	
	รองเท้า		ใหญ่	
	shoes		large	

PATTERN PRACTICE 3:

■ Can I try it on?

Lawng	*dâi-mái?*
ลอง	ได้ไหม
Try on	can...?

■ Yes, you can. / No, you can't.

Lawng	*dâi.*
ลอง	ได้
Try on	can.
	mâi-dâi.
	ไม่ได้
	cannot.

PATTERN PRACTICE 4:

■ Can you lower the price?

Lót	*dâi-mái?*
ลด	ได้ไหม
Discount	can...?

■ I can offer a . . . baht discount.

Lót	**dâi . . . baht.**
ลด	ได้. . .บาท
Discount	can . . . baht.
	mâi-dâi.
	ไม่ได้
	cannot.

Exercises

EXERCISE 1: *Listen and repeat*

sà-bòu nùeng kâwn   a bar of soap
สบู่ 1 ก้อน

praeng-sĭi-fan nùeng an   a toothbrush
แปรงสีฟัน 1 อัน

yaa-sĭi-fan nùeng làwt   a tube of toothpaste
ยาสีฟัน 1 หลอด

yaa-sà-phŏm nùeng khùat   a bottle of shampoo
ยาสระผม 1 ขวด

sûea sǎwng tua   two shirts
เสื้อ 2 ตัว

kaang-keng sǎwng tua   two pairs of pants
กางเกง 2 ตัว

krà-prong sǎwng tua   two skirts
กระโปรง 2 ตัว

krà-pǎo sǎwng bai   two purses
กระเป๋า 2 ใบ

rawng-tháo săwng khôu	two pairs of shoes
รองเท้า 2 คู่	
thŭng-tháo săwng khôu	two pairs of socks
ถุงเท้า 2 คู่	
pàak-kaa săam dâam	three pens
ปากกา 3 ด้าม	
din-săw săam thâeng	three pencils
ดินสอ 3 แท่ง	
sà-mùt săam lêm	three notebooks
สมุด 3 เล่ม	
năng-sŭe săam lêm	three books
หนังสือ 3 เล่ม	
praeng-sĭi-fan an yài	a large toothbrush
แปรงสีฟัน อันใหญ่	
yaa-sĭi-fan làwt lék	a small toothpaste
ยาสีฟัน หลอดเล็ก	
sûea sĭi khăaw	a white shirt
เสื้อ สีขาว	
kaang-keng sĭi dam tua yài	large black pants
กางเกง สีดำ ตัวใหญ่	
krà-prong sĭi daeng tua lék	a small red skirt
กระโปรง สีแดง ตัวเล็ก	
pàak-kaa sĭi nám-ngoen	a blue pen
ปากกา สีน้ำเงิน	
din-săw thâeng yài	a large pencil
ดินสอ แท่งใหญ่	

sà-mùt lêm lék สมุด เล่มเล็ก	small notebook
Súe à-rai? ซื้อ อะไร	Yes, please? (*Lit:* What would you like to buy?)
Súe sûea nùeng tua. ซื้อ เสื้อ 1 ตัว	I want to buy a shirt.
Mii kaang-keng tua yài mái? มี กางเกง ตัวใหญ่ ไหม	Do you have any large pants?
Mii rawng-tháo sïi khǎaw mái? มี รองเท้า สีขาว ไหม	Do you have white shoes?
Mii. / Mâi-mii. มี / ไม่มี	Yes I do. / No, I don't.
Thôa-rài khá/kráp? เท่าไร คะ / ครับ	How much is it?
Sûea thôa-rài? เสื้อ เท่าไร	How much is the shirt?
Lawng dâi-mái? ลอง ได้ไหม	Can I try it on?
Lawng dâi. ลอง ได้	Yes, you can.
Lawng mâi-dâi. ลอง ไม่ได้	No, you can't.
Lót dâi-mái? ลด ได้ไหม	Can you lower the price?
Lót dâi . . . bàat. ลด ได้ . . . บาท	I can offer a . . . baht discount.
Lót mâi-dâi. ลด ไม่ได้	No, I can't.

EXERCISE 2: Number the items from 1–10 as you hear them.

6.09

3 purses _____   a tube of toothpaste _____

2 shirts _____   a bottle of shampoo _____

4 pairs of socks _____   2 pairs of pink pants _____

4 pairs of green shoes _____   3 pens _____

a toothbrush _____   2 yellow skirts _____

EXERCISE 3: Listen and circle the sentence you hear.

6.10

1. a. How much is it?

    b. What would you like to buy?

2. a. I want to buy a skirt.

    b. I want to buy a purse.

3. a. Do you have white pants?

    b. Do you have green pants?

4. a. Can I try it on?

    b. Can you lower the price?

Cultural Notes

✪ Shopping and bargaining

Thailand is a great place for shopping as you can find lots of mega shopping malls, local markets, night markets, department stores, and independent boutiques. You can buy many things that are cheap in price but not necessarily cheap in quality. If you want to buy something from a market or small store it is common to bargain down the price. If you attempt to bargain in Thai, you may get special discount and probably some free gifts. But it is not done in department stores or upscale shops. You also shouldn't bargain with food vendors on the street. It's best to find out the price before you order your food.

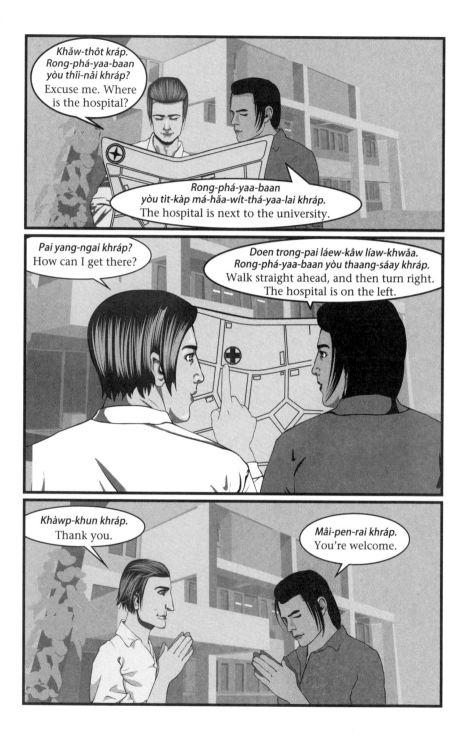

LESSON 7
Directions

In this lesson you will learn how to ask for directions and describe locations using prepositions of place.

DIALOGUE: *Listen and repeat*

Jim: *Khăw-thôt kráp. Rong-phá-yaa-baan yòu thîi-năi khráp?*
ขอโทษ ครับ โรงพยาบาล อยู่ ที่ไหน ครับ
Excuse me. Where is the hospital?

Man: *Rong-phá-yaa-baan yòu tìt-kàp má-hăa-wít-thá-yaa-lai khráp.*
โรงพยาบาล อยู่ ติดกับ มหาวิทยาลัย ครับ
The hospital is next to the university.

Jim: *Yòu klai mái khráp?*
อยู่ ไกล ไหม ครับ
Is it far?

Man: *Mâi-klai khráp.*
ไม่ไกล ครับ
It's not far.

Jim: *Pai yang-ngai khráp?*
ไป ยังไง ครับ
How can I get there?

Man: *Doen trong-pai láew-kâw líaw-khwăa. Rong-phá-yaa-baan yòu thaang-sáay khráp.*
เดิน ตรงไป แล้วก็ เลี้ยวขวา โรงพยาบาล อยู่ ทางซ้าย ครับ
Walk straight ahead, and then turn right. The hospital is on the left.

Jim: **Khàwp-khun khráp.**
ขอบคุณ ครับ
Thank you.

Man: **Mâi-pen-rai khráp.**
ไม่เป็นไร ครับ
You're welcome.

7.02

Asking about locations *Listen and repeat*

khǎw-thôt	ขอโทษ	excuse me
ráan-nǎng-sǔe	ร้านหนังสือ	bookstore
ráan-aa-hǎan	ร้านอาหาร	restaurant
ráan-khǎay-yaa	ร้านขายยา	drugstore
rong-nǎng	โรงหนัง	movie theater
rong-raem	โรงแรม	hotel
rong-phá-yaa-baan	โรงพยาบาล	hospital
thá-naa-khaan	ธนาคาร	bank
prai-sà-nii	ไปรษณีย์	post office
sà-thǎa-nii-tam-rùat	สถานีตำรวจ	police station
má-hǎa-wít-thá-yaa-lai	มหาวิทยาลัย	university
thà-nǒn	ถนน	street, road
rót-sǎwng-thǎew	รถสองแถว	two-row minibus
nâng	นั่ง	take (transport)

khûen	ขึ้น	get on
long	ลง	get off
doen	เดิน	walk
yòu	อยู่	to be
sǎay	สาย	number (only for bus)

Giving directions *Listen and repeat*

⇧	***doen-trong-pai*** เดินตรงไป	go straight ahead
⤺	***líaw-sáay*** เลี้ยวซ้าย	turn left
⇗	***líaw-khwǎa*** เลี้ยวขวา	turn right

◀	***thaang-sáay*** ทางซ้าย	on the left
▶	***thaang-khwǎa*** ทางขวา	on the right

Prepositions of place *Listen and repeat*

trong-khâam	ตรงข้าม	across from
rá-wàang	ระหว่าง	between
tìt-kàp	ติดกับ	next to
hǔa-mum	หัวมุม	on the corner of
thîi	ที่	at
klâi	ใกล้	near/close to
klai	ไกล	far from

QUESTION WORDS: *Listen and repeat*

7.05

... thîi-nǎi?	... ที่ไหน	Where...?
... mái?	... ไหม	Are you...? / Is it...?
... yang-ngai?	... ยังไง	How...?

PATTERN PRACTICE 1:

- Excuse me. Where is the bookstore?

Khǎw-thôt khâ/khráp.	*Ráan-nǎng-sǔe*	*yòu*	*thîi-nǎi?*
ขอโทษ ค่ะ / ครับ	ร้านหนังสือ	อยู่	ที่ไหน
Excuse me.	Bookstore	is	where?
	Prai-sà-nii		
	ไปรษณีย์		
	Post office		
	Ráan-aa-hǎan		
	ร้านอาหาร		
	Restaurant		

- The bookstore is near the bank.

Ráan-nǎng-sǔe	*yòu*	*klâi*	*thá-naa-khaan.*
ร้านหนังสือ	อยู่	ใกล้	ธนาคาร
Bookstore	is	near	bank.
Prai-sà-nii		*trong-khâam*	*ráan-khǎay-yaa.*
ไปรษณีย์		ตรงข้าม	ร้านขายยา
Post office		across from	drugstore.
Ráan-aa-hǎan		*tìt-kàp*	*rong-phá-yaa-baan.*
ร้านอาหาร		ติดกับ	โรงพยาบาล
Restaurant		next to	hospital.

■ The bookstore is between the bank and the restaurant.

Ráan-năng-sǔe	*yòu*	*rá-wàang*	*thá-naa-khaan*	*kàp*	*ráan-aa-hǎan.*
ร้านหนังสือ	อยู่	ระหว่าง	ธนาคาร	กับ	ร้านอาหาร
Bookstore	is	between	bank	and	restaurant.
Prai-sà-nii			*ráan-khǎay-yaa*		*rong-phá-yaa-baan.*
ไปรษณีย์			ร้านขายยา		โรงพยาบาล
Post office			drugstore		hospital.

■ The bookstore is on the left.

Ráan-năng-sǔe	*yòu*	*thaang-sáay.*
ร้านหนังสือ	อยู่	ทางซ้าย
Bookstore	is	on the left.
Prai-sà-nii		*thaang-khwǎa.*
ไปรษณีย์		ทางขวา
Post office		on the right.

PATTERN PRACTICE 2:

■ Is the bookstore far from here?

Ráan-năng-sǔe	*yòu*	*klai*	*mái?*
ร้านหนังสือ	อยู่	ไกล	ไหม
Bookstore	is	far	is it…?
Prai-sà-nii		*klâi*	
ไปรษณีย์		ใกล้	
Post office		near.	

PATTERN PRACTICE 3:

■ How can I get to the bookstore?

Ráan-nǎng-sǔe	*pai*	*yang-ngai?*
ร้านหนังสือ	ไป	ยังไง
Bookstore	go	how?

Prai-sà-nii
ไปรษณีย์
Post office

Ráan-aa-hǎan
ร้านอาหาร
Restaurant

■ Walk straight ahead, then turn left. The bookstore is on the right.

Doen trong-pai	*láew-kâw*	*líaw-sáay.*	*Ráan-nǎng-sǔe*	*yòu*	*thaang-khwǎa.*
เดินตรงไป	แล้วก็	เลี้ยวซ้าย	ร้านหนังสือ	อยู่	ทางขวา
Walk straight	then	turn left.	Bookstore	is	on the right.
Líaw-khwǎa	*thîi*	*hǔa-mum.*	*Prai-sà-nii*		*thaang-sáay.*
เลี้ยวขวา	ที่	หัวมุม	ไปรษณีย์		ทางซ้าย
Turn right	at	the corner.	Post office		on the left.

■ Take songthaew (two-row minibus) No.4.

Nâng	*rót-sǎwng-thǎew*	*sǎay*	*sì*
นั่ง *	รถสองแถว	สาย	4
Take	songthaew	number (only for bus)	4.

Khûen		*sǐ*	*khǐaw*
ขึ้น		สี	เขียว
Get on		color	green.

* *nâng* literally means to sit in the bus.

Grammar Corner

✪ **The verb "to be"**

The verb *yòu* means to live or stay, and also to occupy a specified position or location. It always comes after the subject.

Question: subject + *yòu* + question word?

Answer: subject + *yòu* + preposition + position/location

Q: *Rong-phá-yaa-baan yòu thîi-nǎi?*
โรงพยาบาล อยู่ ที่ไหน

Where is the hospital?

A: *Rong-phá-yaa-baan yòu klâi ráan-khǎay-yaa.*
โรงพยาบาล อยู่ ใกล้ ร้านขายยา

The hospital is near the drugstore.

Exercises

7.06

EXERCISE 1: *Listen and repeat*

Khǎw-thôt khâ/khráp.
ขอโทษ ค่ะ / ครับ

Excuse me.

Prai-sà-nii yòu thîi-nǎi?
ไปรษณีย์ อยู่ ที่ไหน

Where is the post office?

Prai-sà-nii yòu klâi ráan-khǎay-yaa.
ไปรษณีย์ อยู่ ใกล้ ร้านขายยา

The post office is near the drugstore.

Prai-sà-nii yòu trong-khâam thá-naa-khaan.
ไปรษณีย์ อยู่ ตรงข้าม ธนาคาร

The post office is across from the bank.

Prai-sà-nii yòu rá-wàang ráan-aa-hǎan kàp ráan-nǎng-sǔe.
ไปรษณีย์ อยู่ ระหว่าง ร้านอาหาร กับ ร้านหนังสือ

The post office is between the restaurant and the bookstore.

Prai-sà-nii yòu thaang-sáay.
ไปรษณีย์ อยู่ ทาง ซ้าย

The post office is on the left.

Prai-sà-nii yòu thaang-khwǎa. ไปรษณีย์ อยู่ ทาง ขวา	The post office is on the right.
Ráan-khǎay-yaa yòu klai mái? ร้านขายยา อยู่ ไกล ไหม	Is the drugstore far?
Klai. / Mâi-klai. ไกล / ไม่ไกล	It's far. / It's not far.
Rong-raem Sofitel pai yang-ngai? โรงแรม โซฟิเทล ไป ยังไง	How can I get to the hotel Sofitel?
Nâng rót-sǎwng-thǎew sǎay pàet. Láew kâw long thîi thá-naa-khaan. นั่ง รถสองแถว สาย 8 แล้วก็ ลง ที่ ธนาคาร	Take the No.8 songthaew and get off at the bank.
Ráan-aa-hǎan pai yang-ngai? ร้านอาหาร ไป ยังไง	How can I get to the restaurant?
Doen trong-pai láew-kâw líaw-khwǎa. Ráan-aa-hǎan yòu thaang-sáay. เดินตรงไป แล้วก็ เลี้ยวขวา ร้านอาหาร อยู ทางซ้าย	Walk straight ahead, then turn right. The restaurant is on the left.

EXERCISE 2: Write the place names.

Where can you find these things? Write the places in Thai and then practice saying them.

1. aspirin   _____

2. stamps   _____

3. dictionary   _____

4. ATM   _____

5. sandwiches   _____

6. a Harry Potter movie   _____

EXERCISE 3: Translate this dialogue into Thai, then practice.

> A: How do you get to the movie theater?
>
> B: Take the number 28 songthaew and get off at the university. Then walk straight ahead and turn right at the police station. The movie theater is across from the drugstore.

Cultural Notes

✪ **Travel and transport**

Transportation in Thailand is varied and chaotic, but affordable. If you are traveling in Bangkok, then taking a taxi can be a convenient and inexpensive way to get around. Most taxis in Thailand run on meters now, but it's still a good idea to check if the taxi has a running meter before you get in.

Tuk tuks and motorbike taxis are also available in Bangkok and large cities. They cost less than typical taxis, but are considerably less safe. If you decide to use either of these types of transportation, make sure that you negotiate a price in advance.

For travel within large provincial cities, public transport is typically supplied by **sǎwng-thǎew** (**two-row minibus**). Its name is from the two bench seats fixed along either side of the back of the truck. Additionally a roof is fitted over the rear of the vehicle, to which curtains and plastic sheeting to keep out rain may be attached. Songthaews are used both within towns and cities and for longer routes between towns and villages.

The train is a good way to travel around the country. It is by far the safest and most economical form of transport.

LESSON 8
How are you today?

In this lesson you will learn how to ask others about their feelings and talk about your own.

DIALOGUE: *Listen and repeat*

8.01

Teacher: ***Khun Jim sà-baay-dii rúe-plào khá?***
คุณจิม สบายดี หรือเปล่า คะ
Are you all right, Jim?

Jim: ***Phŏm sà-baay-dii khráp.***
ผม สบายดี ครับ
I'm fine.

Teacher: ***Rian phaa-sǎa-thai pen-yang-ngai bâang khá?***
เรียน ภาษาไทย เป็นยังไง บ้าง คะ
How is Thai class?

Jim: ***Rian phaa-sǎa-thai sà-nùk mâak khráp.***
เรียน ภาษาไทย สนุก มาก ครับ
Thai class is really fun.

Teacher: ***Khun Jim nùeay mái khá?***
คุณจิม เหนื่อย ไหม คะ
Are you tired?

Jim: ***Phŏm mâi nùeay loei khráp.***
ผม ไม่ เหนื่อย เลย ครับ
I'm not tired at all.

Feelings *Listen and repeat*

sà-baay-dii	สบายดี	fine, good
sà-nùk	สนุก	fun
nùeay	เหนื่อย	tired
ngûang-nawn	ง่วงนอน	sleepy
bùea	เบื่อ	bored
aay	อาย	shy
klua	กลัว	scared
kròt	โกรธ	angry
tùen-tên	ตื่นเต้น	excited
dii-jai	ดีใจ	happy
sĭa-jai	เสียใจ	sad
ráwn	ร้อน	hot
năow	หนาว	cold
nít-nòy	นิดหน่อย	a bit
mâak	มาก	very
mâi...loei	ไม่...เลย	not...at all

QUESTION WORDS: *Listen and repeat*

pen-yang-ngai	เป็นยังไง	How...?
măi	ไหม	Are you...? / Is it...?
rúe-plào	หรือเปล่า	Are you...? / Is it...?

PATTERN PRACTICE 1:

- How are you?

Khun	*pen-yang-ngai*	*bâang.*
คุณ	เป็นยังไง	บ้าง*
You	how?	else

*Note: The word *bâang* is placed after a question word when more than one answer to the question is possible.

PATTERN PRACTICE 2:

- Are you tired?

Khun	*nùeay*	*mái?*
คุณ	เหนื่อย	ไหม
You	tired	are?
	tùen-tên	*rúe-plào?*
	ตื่นเต้น	หรือเปล่า
	excited	are?
	sà-baay-dii	
	สบายดี	
	fine	

PATTERN PRACTICE 3:

- I am tired.

Chăn/phŏm	*nùeay.*
ฉัน / ผม	เหนื่อย
I	tired.
	tùen-tên.
	ตื่นเต้น
	excited.
	sà-baay-dii.
	สบายดี
	fine.

PATTERN PRACTICE 4:

■ I am a bit tired.

Chăn/phŏm	*nùeay*	*nít-nòy.*
ฉัน / ผม	เหนื่อย	นิดหน่อย
I	tired	a bit
	sĭa-jai	*mâak.*
	เสียใจ	มาก
	sad	very.
	tùen-tên	
	ตื่นเต้น	
	excited	

PATTERN PRACTICE 5:

■ I am not tired at all.

Chăn/phŏm	*mâi*	*nùeay*	*loei.*
ฉัน / ผม	ไม่	เหนื่อย	เลย
I	not	tired	at all
		sĭa-jai	
		เสียใจ	
		sad	
		bùea	
		เบื่อ	
		bored	

Grammar Corner

✪ **Are/Is . . . or not?**

As seen in Lesson 2, the word *mái* can be interpreted as both a general yes/no question and an invitation or suggestion. It is placed at the end of a sentence. To answer "yes," repeat the verb or adjective. To say "no," put *mái* before the verb or adjective.

The phrase **rúe-plào** at the end of statement means "or not?", but unlike English indicates only that you want a definite answer. However, it can be answered in a similar way to the **mái** question and can be used alternatively.

Questions	Form	Yes.	No.
mái ไหม	subject + verb/ adjective + **mái**	subject + verb/adjective	subject + **mâi** (no) + verb/adjective
rúe-plào หรือเปล่า	subject + verb/ adjective + **rúe-plào**	subject + verb/adjective	subject + **mâi** (no) + verb/adjective

Examples:

Questions	Meaning	Yes.	No.
Khun tùen-tên mái? คุณ ตื่นเต้น ไหม	Are you excited?	**Chăn tùen-tên.** ฉัน ตื่นเต้น I'm excited.	**Chăn mâi tùen-tên.** ฉัน ไม่ ตื่นเต้น I'm not excited.
Khun ngûang-nawn rúe-plào? คุณ ง่วงนอน หรือเปล่า	Are you sleepy or not?	**Chăn ngûang-nawn.** ฉัน ง่วงนอน I'm sleepy.	**Chăn mâi ngûang-nawn.** ฉัน ไม่ ง่วงนอน I'm not sleepy.

Exercises

EXERCISE 1: *Listen and repeat*

8.04

Wan-níi khun pen-yang-ngai bâang? วันนี้ คุณ เป็นยังไง บ้าง

How are you today?

Wan-níi chăn/phŏm nùeay. วันนี้ ฉัน / ผม เหนื่อย

I am tired today.

Khun sà-baay-dii mái/rúe-plào?
คุณ สบายดี ไหม / หรือเปล่า
Are you all right?

Chǎn/phǒm sà-baay-dii.
ฉัน / ผม สบายดี
Yes, I am.

Khun klua mái/rúe-plào?
คุณ กลัว ไหม / หรือเปล่า
Are you scared?

Chǎn/phǒm klua.
ฉัน / ผม กลัว
I am scared.

Chǎn/phǒm mâi klua.
ฉัน / ผม ไม่ กลัว
I am not scared.

Khun tùen-tên mái/rúe-plào?
คุณ ตื่นเต้น ไหม / หรือเปล่า
Are you excited?

Chǎn/phǒm tùen-tên nít-nòy.
ฉัน / ผม ตื่นเต้น นิดหน่อย
I am a bit excited.

Chǎn/phǒm mâi tùen-tên loei.
ฉัน / ผม ไม่ ตื่นเต้น เลย
I am not excited at all.

Rian phaa-sǎa-thai sà-nùk mái/rúe-plào?   Is Thai class fun?
เรียน ภาษาไทย สนุก ไหม / หรือ
เปล่า

Rian phaa-sǎa-thai sà-nùk mâak.   Thai class is great
เรียน ภาษาไทย สนุก มาก   (*lit.*very) fun.

Rian phaa-sǎa-thai mâi sà-nùk loei.   Thai class is not fun at all.
เรียน ภาษาไทย ไม่ สนุก เลย

Nùeay mái/rúe-plào?   Are you tired?
เหนื่อย ไหม / หรือเปล่า

Nùeay.   I am tired.
เหนื่อย

Nùeay nít-nòy.   I am a bit tired.
เหนื่อย นิดหน่อย

Nùeay mâak.   I am very tired.
เหนื่อย มาก

Mâi nùeay.   I am not tired.
ไม่ เหนื่อย

Mâi nùeay loei.   I am not tired at all.
ไม่ เหนื่อย เลย

*Note: the final six sentences above are given without personal pronouns for a more informal way of speaking.

EXERCISE 2: Listen to the questions and write your own answers.

8.05

1. _____

2. _____

3. _____

4. _____

5. _____

EXERCISE 3: How do you say these sentences in Thai?

1. How are you today?

_____

2. Thai class is fun. I'm excited and happy.

_____

3. My younger sister is not shy at all.

_____

4. I am bored today.

_____

5. Do you feel cold?

_____

Cultural Notes

✪ **How are you?**

Sà-baay-dii mái is a common Thai greeting that's typically translated as "How are you?", though a more literal translation would be, "Is everything well and good?" The standard reply is *sà-baay-dii*, or an affirmative "well and good." When saying *sà-baay-dii*, it can convey not only a sense of stability, peace, and happiness, but also of physical wellness.

In some cases, the word is often repeated twice, as in *sà-baay sà-baay*, to emphasize that everything is really just great and couldn't be better. You'll also hear *sà-baay sà-baay* used as a way to describe a relaxing environment.

LESSON 9
Health

In this lesson you will learn how to describe your health and ailments.

DIALOGUE: *Listen and repeat*

9.01

Malee: ***Khun Jim pen-yang-ngai bâang khá?***
คุณจิม เป็นยังไง บ้าง คะ
How are you, Jim?

Jim: ***Phǒm mâi sà-baay khráp.***
ผม ไม่สบาย ครับ
I'm not feeling well.

Malee: ***Khun pen à-rai khá?***
คุณ เป็นอะไร คะ
What's wrong?

Jim: ***Phǒm pùat-hǔa khráp.***
ผม ปวดหัว ครับ
I have a headache.

Malee: ***Khun Jim kin-yaa rúe-yang khá?***
คุณจิม กินยา หรือยัง คะ
Have you taken any medicine?

Jim: ***Kin láew khráp.***
กิน แล้ว ครับ
Yes, I've taken some already.

Malee: ***Khun Jim tâwng phák-phàwn khâ.***
คุณจิม ต้อง พักผ่อน ค่ะ
You must get some rest.

9.02

Body parts *Listen and repeat*

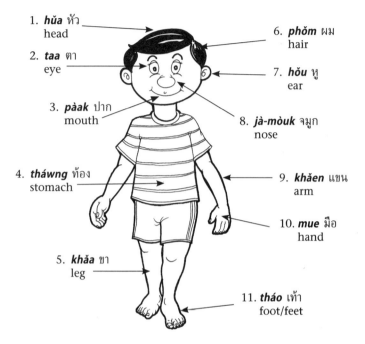

1. *hǔa* หัว
   head
2. *taa* ตา
   eye
3. *pàak* ปาก
   mouth
4. *tháwng* ท้อง
   stomach
5. *khǎa* ขา
   leg

6. *phǒm* ผม
   hair
7. *hǒu* หู
   ear
8. *jà-mòuk* จมูก
   nose
9. *khǎen* แขน
   arm
10. *mue* มือ
    hand
11. *tháo* เท้า
    foot/feet

9.03

Health problems *Listen and repeat*

pen-wàt	เป็นหวัด	a cold
pen-khâi	เป็นไข้	a fever
pùat-hǔa	ปวดหัว	a headache
pùat-fan	ปวดฟัน	a toothache
pùat-tháwng	ปวดท้อง	a stomachache
pùat-lǎng	ปวดหลัง	a backache

jèp-taa	เจ็บตา	sore eyes
jèp-khaw	เจ็บคอ	a sore throat
ai	ไอ	a cough
aa-jian	อาเจียน	vomiting
tháwng-sĭa	ท้องเสีย	diarrhea
pen-phùen	เป็นผื่น	skin rash

Giving advice *Listen and repeat*

9.04

mâi-sà-baay	ไม่สบาย	get sick, not feel well
tâwng	ต้อง	have to, must
kin-yaa	กินยา	take some medicine
phák-phàwn	พักผ่อน	get some rest
pai-hăa-măw	ไปหาหมอ	go see the doctor
...láew	...แล้ว	already
yang-mâi-dâi...	ยังไม่ได้...	haven't yet

CONVERSATION QUESTIONS: *Listen and repeat*

9.05

| Khun pen à-rai? | คุณ เป็นอะไร | What's wrong? |
| ...rúe-yang? | หรือยัง | Have you ... yet? |

PATTERN PRACTICE 1:

■ How are you?

Khun	**pen-yang-ngai**	**bâang?**
คุณ	เป็นยังไง	บ้าง*
You	how?	else

*Note: **(bâang)** บ้าง is placed after a question word when more than one answer to the question is possible.

■ I am sick.

Chăn/phŏm	**mâi-sà-baay.**
ฉัน / ผม	ไม่สบาย
I	get sick.

PATTERN PRACTICE 2:

■ What's wrong?

Khun	**pen à-rai?**
คุณ	เป็นอะไร
You	what's wrong?

■ I have a cold

Chăn/phŏm	**pen-wàt.**
ฉัน / ผม	เป็นหวัด
I	a cold.
	pùat-tháwng.
	ปวดท้อง
	a stomachache.
	pùat-hŭa.
	ปวดหัว
	a headache.

PATTERN PRACTICE 3:

- Have you taken any medicine?

Khun	**kin-yaa**	**rúe-yang?**
คุณ	กินยา	หรือยัง
You	take some medicine	have you yet?
	pai-hǎa-mǎw	
	ไปหาหมอ	
	go see the doctor	

- Yes, I've taken some already.

Chǎn/phǒm	**kin-yaa**	**láew.**
ฉัน / ผม	กินยา	แล้ว
I	take some medicine	already.
	pai-hǎa-mǎw	
	ไปหาหมอ	
	go see the doctor	

- No, I haven't taken any yet.

Chǎn/phǒm	**yang-mâi-dâi**	**kin-yaa.**
ฉัน / ผม	ยังไม่ได้	กินยา
I	haven't yet	take some medicine.
		pai-hǎa-mǎw.
		ไปหาหมอ
		go see the doctor.

PATTERN PRACTICE 4:

■ You have to get some rest.

Khun	tâwng	phák-phàwn.
คุณ	ต้อง	พักผ่อน
you	have to	get some rest.
		kin-yaa.
		กินยา
		take some medicine.
		pai-hǎa-mǎw.
		ไปหาหมอ
		go see the doctor.

Grammar Corner

✪ **Have you . . . yet?**

The phrase **rúe-yang** is used to ask whether one has done something previously or has done something yet. It is always placed at the end of a sentence.

- To answer "yes" put **láew** (already) after the verb.

- To say "no" put **yang-mâi-dâi** (not yet) before the verb.

Question: subject + verb + (object) + **rúe-yang**

Yes: subject + verb + (object) + **láew**

No: subject + **yang-mâi-dâi** + verb + (object)

Example:

Questions	Yes.	No.
Khun kin-yaa rúe-yang? คุณ กินยา หรือยัง Have you taken any medicine?	**Chăn kin láew.** ฉัน กิน แล้ว I've taken some already.	**Chăn yang-mâi-dâi kin.** ฉัน ยังไม่ได้ กิน I haven't taken any yet.
Khun àap-nám rúe-yang? คุณ อาบน้ำ หรือยัง Have you taken a bath yet?	**Phŏm àap-nám láew.** ผม อาบน้ำ แล้ว I've taken a bath already.	**Phŏm yang-mâi-dâi àap-nám.** ผม ยังไม่ได้ อาบน้ำ I haven't taken a bath yet.

Exercises

EXERCISE 1: *Listen and repeat*

9.06

✪ Health problems

Khun pen-yang-ngai bâang?   How are you?
คุณ เป็นยังไง บ้าง

Chăn/phŏm mâi sà-baay.   I am sick.
ฉัน / ผม ไม่สบาย

Khun pen à-rai?
คุณ เป็นอะไร

What's wrong?

Khun kin-yaa rúe-yang?
คุณ กินยา หรือยัง

Have you taken any medicine?

Chǎn/phǒm kin-yaa láew.
ฉัน / ผม กินยา แล้ว

Yes, I've taken some already.

Chǎn/phǒm yang-mâi-dâi kin-yaa.
ฉัน / ผม ยังไม่ได้ กินยา

No, I haven't taken any yet.

Khun pai-hǎa-mǎw rúe-yang?
คุณ ไปหาหมอ หรือยัง

Have you seen the doctor?

Chǎn/phǒm pai-hǎa-mǎw láew.
ฉัน / ผม ไปหาหมอ แล้ว

Yes, I've seen the doctor already.

Chǎn/phǒm yang-mâi-dâi pai-hǎa-mǎw.
ฉัน / ผม ยังไม่ได้ ไปหาหมอ

No, I haven't seen the doctor yet.

✪ Giving advice

Khun tâwng phák-phàwn.
คุณ ต้อง พักผ่อน

You have to get some rest.

Khun tâwng kin-yaa.
คุณ ต้อง กินยา

You have to take some medicine.

Khun tâwng pai-hǎa-mǎw.
คุณ ต้อง ไปหาหมอ

You have to go to see the doctor.

EXERCISE 2: Translate the following dialogues into Thai.

1. A : Have you seen the doctor?
   B : Yes, I have seen the doctor already.

2. A : How are you?
   B : I'm not feeling well.

3. A : I have a headache.
   B : You have to get some rest.

4. A : What's wrong?
   B : I have a cold

5. A : Have you taken any medicine?
   B : I haven't taken any medicine yet

Cultural Notes

♻ **Body parts**

In Thai culture, different body parts are worthy of different levels of respect. Remember that Thais dislike being touched anywhere, and that they place special emphasis on the head, the hands, and the feet.

<u>Head:</u> The head is considered the most respected and the most important part of the entire body. You should never touch anyone's head for any reason.

<u>Hands:</u> Don't point with the forefinger at anyone. Also, it is more acceptable and polite to use the right hand when giving and receiving things, and putting things into the mouth. This is because the left hand is used to clean oneself after going to the toilet.

<u>Feet:</u> The feet are considered the dirtiest part of the body because they are in contact with the ground. Therefore, don't point your feet (with or without shoes on) towards a person, or religious image or a picture of the royal family. Also, don't use your feet to move anything or touch anyone. Lastly, you should not step over any part of the body of a person that is lying down.

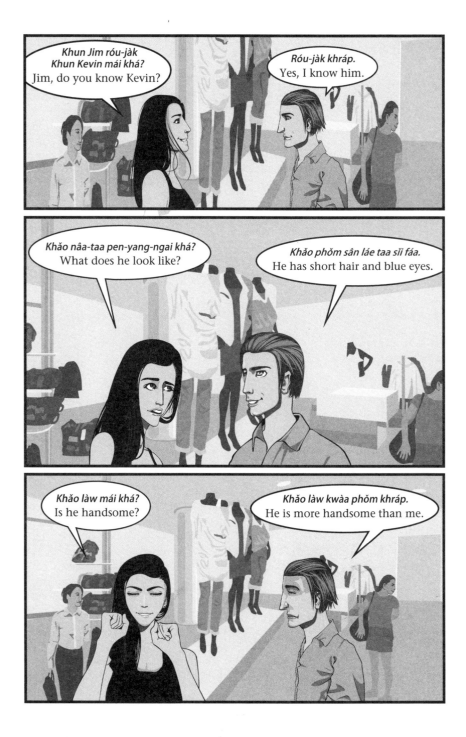

LESSON 10
Describing people

In this lesson you will learn how to describe people's appearance and personality.

DIALOGUE: *Listen and repeat*

Malee: **Khun Jim róu-jàk Khun Kevin mái khá?**
คุณจิม รู้จัก คุณเควิน ไหม คะ
Jim, do you know Kevin?

Jim: **Róu-jàk khráp.**
รู้จัก ครับ
Yes, I know him.

Malee: **Khǎo nâa-taa pen-yang-ngai khá?**
เขา หน้าตา เป็นยังไง คะ
What does he look like?

Jim: **Khǎo phǒm sân láe taa sǐi fáa.**
เขา ผม สั้น และ ตา สีฟ้า
He has short hair and blue eyes.

Malee: **Khǎo làw mái khá?**
เขา หล่อ ไหม คะ
Is he handsome?

Jim: **Khǎo làw kwàa phǒm khráp.**
เขา หล่อ กว่า ผม ครับ
He is more handsome than me.

Malee: ***Khǎo pen khon yang-ngai ká?***
เขา เป็น คน ยังไง คะ
What is he like?

Jim: ***Khǎo jai-dii láe khà-yǎn thîi-sùt khráp.***
เขา ใจดี และ ขยัน ที่สุด ครับ
He is kind and extremely hardworking.

10.02

Appearance Listen and repeat

nâa	หน้า	face
taa	ตา	eyes
jà-mòuk	จมูก	nose
pàak	ปาก	mouth
hǒu	หู	ears
phǒm	ผม	hair
sân	สั้น	short
yaaw	ยาว	long
lék	เล็ก	small
yài	ใหญ่	big
oûan	อ้วน	fat
phǎwm	ผอม	thin, skinny
sǒung	สูง	tall
tîa	เตี้ย	short (height)
sǔay	สวย	beautiful (women only)
làw	หล่อ	handsome (men only)

nâa-rák	น่ารัก	cute
khăo mii nùat	เขา มี หนวด	He has a moustache
khăo sài-wâen	เขา ใส่แว่น	He wears glasses
khăo mii krao	เขา มี เครา	He has a beard
khăo	เขา	he/she/they
róu-jàk	รู้จัก	know (someone)
nâa-taa	หน้าตา	appearance
láe	และ	and

Personality and characteristics
Listen and repeat

10.03

khà-yăn	ขยัน	hardworking
khîi-kìat	ขี้เกียจ	lazy
khîi-aay	ขี้อาย	shy
khîi-nĭaw	ขี้เหนียว	stingy
râa-roeng	ร่าเริง	cheerful
jai-dii	ใจดี	kind, nice
jai-dam	ใจดำ	unkind, mean
jai-ráwn	ใจร้อน	impatient
jai-yen	ใจเย็น	calm, patient
kèng	เก่ง	skillful, good at
chà-làat	ฉลาด	smart
mâak	มาก	very (used with adjectives)

| ...kwàa | ...กว่า | comparative form of adjectives (more ... than) |
| ...thîi-sùt | ...ที่สุด | superlative form of adjectives (the most ...), extremely |

Question words *Listen and repeat*

10.04

...mái?	...ไหม	Are you...? / Do you...?
...pen-yang-ngai?	...เป็นยังไง	How...?
...pen khon yang-ngai?	...เป็น คน ยังไง	What is ... (person) like?

PATTERN PRACTICE 1:

■ Do you know Jim?

Khun	róu-jàk	Jim	mái?
คุณ	รู้จัก	จิม	ไหม
You	know		do you...?
		Malee	
		มาลี	

PATTERN PRACTICE 2:

■ What does he look like?

Khǎo	nâa-taa	pen-yang-ngai?
เขา	หน้าตา	เป็นยังไง
He/she	appearance	how?

- He/she has short hair.

Khăo	taa	sĭi-dam.
เขา	ตา	สีดำ
He/she	eyes	black/dark.
	phŏm	sân.
	ผม	สั้น
	hair	short.

PATTERN PRACTICE 3:

- Is he handsome? / Is she beautiful?

Khăo	làw	mái?
เขา	หล่อ	ไหม
He/she	handsome	is . . . ?
	sŭay	
	สวย	
	beautiful	
	sŏung	
	สูง	
	tall	

- He is handsome. / She is beautiful.

Khăo	làw.
เขา	หล่อ
He/she	handsome.
	sŭay.
	สวย
	beautiful.
	sŏung.
	สูง
	tall.

PATTERN PRACTICE 4:

■ Does he have a mustache?

Khǎo	*mii*	*nùat*	*mái?*
เขา	มี	หนวด	ไหม
He/she	have	mustache	do/does...?
	sài	*wâen*	
	ใส่	แว่น	
	wear	glasses	

PATTERN PRACTICE 5:

■ What is he like?

Khǎo	*pen khon yang-ngai?*
เขา	เป็น คน ยังไง
He/she	what is ... like?

■ He/she is very kind.

Khǎo	*jai-dii*	*mâak.*
เขา	ใจดี	มาก
He/she	kind	very.
	râa-roeng	
	ร่าเริง	
	cheerful	
	khîi-kiat	
	ขี้เกียจ	
	lazy	

PATTERN PRACTICE 6:

■ She is taller than me.
I'm more hardworking than him.

Khǎo	*sǒung*	*kwàa*	*phǒm.*
เขา	สูง	กว่า	ผม
He/she	tall	more	me.
Phǒm	*làw*	(comparative)	*khǎo.*
ผม	หล่อ		เขา
I	handsome		him/her.
	khà-yǎn		
	ขยัน		
	hardworking		

PATTERN PRACTICE 7:

■ He is the tallest.
She is the most beautiful.

Khǎo	*sǒung*	*thîi-sùt.*
เขา	สูง	ที่สุด
He/she	tall	the most.
Phǒm	*làw*	(superlative)
ผม	หล่อ	
I	handsome	
Chǎn	*sǔay*	
ฉัน	สวย	
I	beautiful	
	khà-yǎn	
	ขยัน	
	hardworking	

Grammar Corner

✪ Comparative and superlative

- The comparative is formed by putting **kwàa** after the adjective or adverb.

  *subject + adjective/adverb + **kwàa** + subject*

- The superlative is formed by putting ***thîi-sùt*** after the adjective or adverb.

  *subject + adjective/adverb + **thîi-sùt***

Example:

Comparative Form	Superlative Form
Anne sŭay kwàa Jane. แอน สวย กว่า เจน Anne is more beautiful than Jane.	***Anne sŭay thîi-sùt*** แอน สวย ที่สุด Anne is extremely beautiful (*lit.* the most beautiful).
Kài-thâwt à-ròi <u>kwàa</u> mŏu-yâang. ไก่ทอด อร่อย กว่า หมูย่าง Fried chicken is more delicious than grilled pork.	***Kài-thâwt à-ròi <u>thîi-sùt</u>.*** ไก่ทอด อร่อย ที่สุด Fried chicken is extremely delicious.

Exercises

EXERCISE 1: *Listen and repeat*

10.05

✪ **Describing a woman**

Khun róu-jàk Malee mái?
คุณ รู้จัก มาลี ไหม

Do you know Malee?

Róu-jàk khâ/khráp.
รู้จัก ค่ะ/ครับ

Yes, I do.

Khǎo nâa-taa pen-yang-ngai? เขา หน้าตา เป็นยังไง	What does she look like?
Khǎo nâa lék. เขา หน้า เล็ก	She has a small face.
Khǎo taa sǐi nám-taan. เขา ตา สีน้ำตาล	She has brown eyes.
Khǎo phǒm yaaw. เขา ผม ยาว	She has long hair.
Khǎo sǔay mái? เขา สวย ไหม	Is she pretty?
Khǎo sǔay. เขา สวย	Yes, she is.
Khǎo sài-wâen mái? เขา ใส่แว่น ไหม	Does she wear glasses?
Khǎo sài-wâen. เขา ใส่แว่น	Yes, she does.
Khǎo mâi-sài-wâen. เขา ไม่ใส่แว่น	No, she doesn't.
Khun Malee pen khon yang-ngai? คุณมาลี เป็น คน ยังไง	What's Malee like?
Khǎo khà-yǎn. เขา ขยัน	She is hardworking.
Khǎo khîi-aay mâak. เขา ขี้อาย มาก	She is very shy.
Khǎo jai-yen kwàa chǎn/phǒm. เขา ใจเย็น กว่า ฉัน/ผม	She is more patient than me.
Khǎo jai-dii thîi-sùt. เขา ใจดี ที่สุด	She is extremely kind (*lit.* she is the kindest).

✪ Describing a man

Khun róu-jàk Khun Jim mái?	Do you know Jim?
คุณ รู้จัก คุณจิม ไหม	
Róu-jàk khâ/khráp.	Yes, I do.
รู้จัก ค่ะ/ครับ	
Khǎo nâa-taa pen-yang-ngai?	What does he look like?
เขา หน้าตา เป็นยังไง	
Khǎo jà-mòuk yài.	He has a big nose.
เขา จมูก ใหญ่	
Khǎo taa sǐi fáa.	He has blue eyes.
เขา ตา สีฟ้า	
Khǎo phǒm sân.	He has short hair.
เขา ผม สั้น	
Khǎo làw mái?	Is he handsome?
เขา หล่อ ไหม	
Khǎo làw.	Yes, he is.
เขา หล่อ	
Khǎo mii nùat mái?	Does he have a moustache?
เขา มี หนวด ไหม	
Khǎo mii nùat.	Yes, he does.
เขา มี หนวด	
Khǎo mâi mii nùat.	No, he doesn't.
เขา ไม่มี หนวด	
Khun Jim pen khon yang-ngai?	What's Jim like?
คุณจิม เป็น คน ยังไง	
Khǎo râa-roeng.	He is cheerful.
เขา ร่าเริง	

Khǎo khîi-aay mâak.	He is very shy.
เขา ขี้อาย มาก	
Khǎo chà-làat kwàa chǎn/phǒm.	He is smarter than me.
เขา ฉลาด กว่า ฉัน/ผม	
Khǎo jai-yen thîi-sùt.	He is extremely calm
เขา ใจเย็น ที่สุด	(*lit.* he is the calmest).

EXERCISE 2: Describe the following people.

1. Jim 2. Malee 3. A friend 4. Yourself

Cultural Notes

✪ **Being called "fat"**

The Thais call overweight people ***oûan*** (fat) as a nickname. Western-ers would consider this rude but the Thais don't mean to hurt your feelings. It's a compliment, as being fat shows that you live well.

✪ **Thai characteristics**

Thai people are friendly. If you are lost, you can ask anyone for directions. Even if those you ask don't know your language, they will do everything to help you. There are two common phrases that convey this easygoing attitude: ***mâi-pen-rai*** and ***jai-yen-yen***.

• The phrase ***mâi-pen-rai*** is equivalent to "never mind"/ "that's OK"/"it doesn't matter"/"no problem." Many Thai people say it because they believe that they don't have much control over things. Just accept and move on.

• The phrase ***jai-yen-yen*** means "take it easy"/"calm down." Thai people always try to avoid direct confrontation and to not place themselves in a situation of potential violence.

Communications

In this lesson, you will learn language for making and answering a phone call, as well as talking about the Internet. You will also learn the phrases and words you need to exchange money and carry out simple banking transactions.

DIALOGUE 1: *Listen and repeat*

11.01

Jim:	***Han-lŏ. Khăw phôut kàp Khun Somsri khráp?***
	ฮัลโหล ขอ พูด กับ คุณสมศรี ครับ
	Hello. May I speak to Somsri, please?

Receptionist: ***Raw-sàk-krôu khâ . . . Khun Somsri mâi-wâang ráp-săay khâ.***
รอสักครู่ ค่ะ คุณสมศรี ไม่ว่าง รับสาย ค่ะ
Hold the line, please . . . I'm afraid she's busy right now.

Jim: ***Khun mii boe mue-thŭe Khun Somsri mái khráp?***
คุณ มี เบอร์ มือถือ คุณสมศรี ไหม ครับ
Do you have her cell phone number?

Receptionist: ***Mâi mii khâ. Khun jà fàk-khâw-khwaam mái khá.***
ไม่มี ค่ะ คุณ จะ ฝากข้อความ ไหม คะ
No, I don't. Would you like to leave a message?

Jim: ***Chûay bàwk Khun Somsri wâa phŏm tho-maa khráp. Hâi-tho-klàp phŏm boe sŏun-pàet-kâo-jèt-săam-săam-hâa-pàet-jèt-sìi. Khàwp-khun khráp.***
ช่วย บอก คุณสมศรี ว่า ผม ครับ โทรมา ครับ ให้ โทรกลับ ผม เบอร์ 089-7335874 ขอบคุณ ครับ
Please tell her that I called and to call me back on 089-7335874. Thank you.

11.02

Making a phone call *Listen and repeat*

han-lǒ	ฮัลโหล	hello (on the phone)
khǎw	ขอ	I'd like.... / May I have....?
phôut	พูด	speak
kam-lang phôut	กำลังพูด	to be speaking
kàp	กับ	with
tho-hǎa	โทรหา	give someone a call
tho-maa	โทรมา	someone called you
hâi-tho-klàp	ให้โทรกลับ	return a call, call back
tho-rá-sàp	โทรศัพท์	phone
boe (tho-rá-sàp)	เบอร์ (โทรศัพท์)	phone number
mue-thǔe	มือถือ	mobile phone
ráp-sǎay	รับสาย	to answer/pick up the phone
waang-sǎay	วางสาย	hang up the phone
sǎay-mâi-wâang	สายไม่ว่าง	the line is busy/engaged
mâi-yòu	ไม่อยู่	(person) is not in
Raw-sàk-krôu.	รอสักครู่	Hold the line, please.
fàk-khâw-khwaam	ฝากข้อความ	leave a message
Chûay bàwk . . . wâa	ช่วยบอก...ว่า	Please tell (someone) that . . .
Mái . . .	ไหม	Do/does...? Would you like...? (offering)

PATTERN PRACTICE 1:

■ Hello. May I speak to Jim, please?

Han-lŏ.	*Khăw*	*phôut*	*kàp*	*Khun Jim?*
ฮัลโหล	ขอ	พูด	กับ	คุณจิม
	May I...?	speak	with	Jim

PATTERN PRACTICE 2:

■ Excuse me. Do you have Jim's mobile phone number?

Khăw-thôt khâ/khráp.	*Mii*	*boe*	*mue-thŭe*	*Khun Jim*	*mái?*
ขอโทษ ค่ะ/ครับ	มี	เบอร์	มือถือ	คุณจิม	ไหม
Excuse me.	Have	number	mobile phone	Jim	do...?
			tho-rá-sàp		
			โทรศัพท์		
			phone		

PATTERN PRACTICE 3:

■ Would you like to leave a message?

Khun	*jà*	*fàk-khâw-khwaam*	*mái?*
คุณ	จะ	ฝากข้อความ	ไหม
you	like to (lit. will)	leave a message	would...?
		hâi-tho-klàp	
		ให้โทรกลับ	
		return your call	

■ Please tell him/her that I called.

Chûay	*bàwk*	*khăo*	*wâa*	*chăn/phŏm*	*tho-maa.*
ช่วย	บอก	เขา	ว่า	ฉัน/ผม	โทรมา
Please	tell	him/her	that	I	give a call.

■ Please tell him/her to call me back on 043-342913

Chûay	bàwk	khăo	hâi-tho-klàp	chăn/phŏm	boe sŏun-sìi-săam-săam-sìi-săwng-kâo-nùeng-săam.
ช่วย	บอก	เขา	ให้โทรกลับ	ฉัน/ผม	ช่วย บอก เขา โทร หา ฉัน เบอร์
Please	tell	him/her	call back	me	number 043-342913.
			tho-hăa		
			โทรหา		
			give a call		

Grammar Corner

❂ **Please**

The word **chûay** can be interpreted as "please." It is usually placed at the beginning of a sentence in order to soften a request or ask for a favor or assistance.

Examples:

Chûay tho-klàp Jim khráp. ช่วย โทรกลับ จิม ครับ	Please call Jim back.
Chûay bàwk khăo tho-hăa chăn boe sŏun-sìi-săam-săam-sìi-săwng-kâo-nùeng-săam khâ. ช่วย บอก เขา โทรหา ฉัน เบอร์ 043-342913	Please tell him/her to give me a call on 043-342913.

11.03

Internet *Listen and repeat*

in-toe-nèt	อินเตอร์เน็ต	Internet
khawm-phíew-tôe	คอมพิวเตอร์	computer/laptop
waay-faay	วาย ฟาย	Wi-Fi connection
ii-meo	อีเมล์	e-mail address
chái	ใช้	use
tàw	ต่อ	connect
khâo	เข้า	get access
rá-hàt	รหัส	password
chék	เช็ค	check
sòng	ส่ง	send
mái	ไหม	Do/does...?
Khǎw . . . dâi-mái?	ขอ...ได้ไหม	Could . . . please? (asking for permission)

PATTERN PRACTICE 4:

■ Do you have a Wi-Fi connection?

Khun	*mii*	*waay-faay*	*mái?*
คุณ	มี	วายฟาย	ไหม
you	have	Wi-Fi	do...?
		khawm-phíew-tôe	
		คอมพิวเตอร์	
		computer	
		ii-meo	
		อีเมล์	
		e-mail	

PATTERN PRACTICE 5:

- Could I get a Wi-Fi password, please?

Khǎw	*rá-hàt*	*waay-faay*	*dâi-mái?*
ขอ	รหัส	วายฟาย	ได้ไหม
please	password	Wi-Fi	could I ...?
	chái	*khawm-phíew-tôe*	
	ใช้	คอมพิวเตอร์	
	use	computer	

PATTERN PRACTICE 6:

- I cannot get access to the Internet.

Chǎn/phǒm	*khâo*	*in-toe-nèt*	*mâi-dâi.*
ฉัน/ผม	เข้า	อินเตอร์เน็ต	ไม่ได้
I	get access	Internet	cannot.
	tàw	*waay-faay*	
	ต่อ	วายฟาย	
	connect	Wi-Fi	
	sòng	*ii-meo*	
	ส่ง	อีเมล์	
	send	e-mail	

Exercises

EXERCISE 1: *Listen and repeat*

11.04

Han-lǒ. Khǎw phôut kàp Khun Jim?
ฮัลโหล ขอ พูด กับ คุณจิม

Hello. May I speak to Jim, please?

Raw-sàk-krôu khâ /khráp.
รอ สักครู่ ค่ะ/ครับ

Hold the line, please.

Mâi-yòu khâ /khráp.
ไม่อยู่ ค่ะ/ครับ

He is not in.

Mâi-wâang ráp-săay khâ /khráp.
ไม่ว่าง รับสาย ค่ะ/ครับ

He is too busy (to answer the phone).

Săay-mâi-wâang khâ /khráp.
สายไม่ว่าง ค่ะ/ครับ

The line is busy at the moment.

Kam-lang phôut khâ /khráp.
กำลังพูด ค่ะ/ครับ

Speaking.

Khăw-thôt khâ /khráp. Khun mii boe mue-thǔe Khun Jim mái?
ขอโทษ ค่ะ/ครับ คุณมี เบอร์ มือถือ คุณจิม ไหม

Excuse me. Do you have Jim's mobile phone number?

Mii khâ/khráp.
มี ค่ะ/ครับ

Yes, I do.

Mâi-mii khâ/khráp.
ไม่มี ค่ะ/ครับ

No, I don't.

Khun jà fàk-khâw-khwaam mái?
คุณ จะ ฝากข้อความ ไหม

Would you like to leave a message?

Chûay bàwk khǎo wâa chǎn/phǒm tho-maa.
ช่วย บอก เขา ว่า ฉัน/ผม โทรมา

Please tell him I called.

Chûay bàwk khǎo hâi-tho-klàp chǎn/ phǒm boe sǒun-pàet- kâo-jèt-săam- sǎam-hâa-pàet-jèt-sìi.
ช่วย บอก เขา ให้โทรกลับ ฉัน/ผม เบอร์ 089-7335874

Please tell him to call me back on 089-7335874.

Khàwp-khun khâ/khráp.
ขอบคุณ ค่ะ/ครับ

Thank you.

Khun mii waay-faay mái?
คุณ มี วายฟาย ไหม

Do you have a Wi-Fi connection?

Khǎw rá-hàt waay-faay dâi-mái?
ขอ รหัส วายฟาย ได้ไหม

Could I get a Wi-Fi password, please?

Chǎn/phǒm khâo in-toe-nèt mâi-dâi.
ฉัน/ผม เข้า อินเตอร์เน็ต ไม่ได้

I cannot get access to the Internet.

EXERCISE 2: Write the correct words in the phone conversations.

1. Jim: Hello. <u>May I speak</u> to Ms. Kaew, please?

   Han-lǒ. _____ *kàp Khun Kaew khráp?*

   Receptionist: Ms. Kaew is <u>not in</u>.

   Khun Kaew _____ *khâ.*

2. Jim: Do you <u>have</u> Mr. Sak's <u>mobile phone</u> number?

   Khun _____ *boe* _____ *Khun Sak mái khráp?*

   Receptionist: Yes, <u>I do</u>.

   _____ *khâ.*

3. Receptionist: Would you like to <u>leave a message</u>?

   Khun jà _____ *khá?*

   Jim: Please <u>tell</u> him that I <u>called</u>.

   Chûay _____ *khǎo wâa phǒm* _____ *khráp.*

11.05

DIALOGUE 2: *Listen and repeat*

Jim: **Phŏm khăw lâek-ngoen săam-rói dawn-lâa khráp.**
ผม ขอ แลกเงิน 300 ดอลล่าร์ ครับ
I'd like to exchange 300 U.S. dollars.

Teller: **Khăw năng-sŭe-doen-thaang dûay khâ.**
ขอ หนังสือเดินทาง ด้วย ค่ะ
May I have your passport too?

Nîi khâ kâo-phan bàat.
นี่ค่ะ 9,000 บาท
Here is 9,000 baht.

Jim: **Phŏm khăw pòet-ban-chii dûay khráp.**
ผม ขอ เปิดบัญชี ด้วย ครับ
I would like to open an account as well.

Teller: **Ban-chii-awm-sáp rŭe krà-săe-raay-wan khá.**
บัญชีออมทรัพย์ หรือ กระแสรายวัน คะ
A savings or a cheque account?

Jim: **Ban-chii-awm-sáp khráp.**
บัญชีออมทรัพย์ ครับ
A savings account, please.

Teller: **Khăw bai-à-nú-yâat-tham-ngaan khâ?**
ขอ ใบอนุญาตทำงาน ค่ะ
May I have your work permit?

Jim: **Nîi khráp.**
นี่ ครับ
Here you are.

Teller: **Khàwp-khun khâ. Chûay khĭan bàep-fawm dûay khâ.**
ขอบคุณค่ะ ช่วย เขียน แบบฟอร์ม ด้วย ค่ะ
Thank you. Please could you fill in this form.

> **Khun jà fàak-ngoen thâo-rài khá.**
>
> คุณ จะ ฝากเงิน เท่าไร คะ
>
> How much do you want to deposit?

Jim: **Săam-phan bàat khráp.**

3,000 บาท ครับ

I would like to deposit 3,000 baht.

At the bank Listen and repeat

11.06

ngoen	เงิน	money, cash
dawn-lâa	ดอลลาร์	dollar
bàat	บาท	baht
lâek-ngoen	แลกเงิน	exchange money
thăwn-ngoen	ถอนเงิน	withdraw
fàak-ngoen	ฝากเงิน	deposit
on-ngoen	โอนเงิน	transfer money
pòet-ban-chii	เปิดบัญชี	open an account
pìt-ban-chii	ปิดบัญชี	close an account
ban-chii-awm-sáp	บัญชีออมทรัพย์	savings account
ban-chii-krà-săe-raay-wan	บัญชีกระแสรายวัน	cheque account/ current account
bàt-e-thii-em	บัตรเอทีเอ็ม	ATM card
bàt-khre-dìt	บัตรเครดิต	credit card
tôu-e-thii-em	ตู้ เอทีเอ็ม	ATM machine
năng-sŭe-doen-thaang	หนังสือเดินทาง	passport

bai-à-nú-yâat-tham-ngaan	ใบอนุญาตทำงาน	work permit
bàep-fawm	แบบฟอร์ม	account application form
khâa	ค่า...	fee/charge
Nîi khâ/khráp.	นี่ ค่ะ/ครับ	Here you are. / Here it is. /This is...
dûay	ด้วย	too, also, as well
jà	จะ	will/shall
...thâo-rài?	...เท่าไร	how much...?

PATTERN PRACTICE 7:

■ How much do you want to exchange?

Khun	jà	lâek-ngoen	thâo-rài?
คุณ	จะ	แลกเงิน	เท่าไร
You	going to	exchange	how much...?
		fàak-ngoen	
		ฝากเงิน	
		deposit	

■ I'd like to exchange 100 U.S. dollars.

Chăn/phŏm	khăw	lâek-ngoen	nùeng-rói	dawn-lâa.
ฉัน/ผม	ขอ	แลกเงิน	100	ดอลลาร์
I	would like	exchange		dollars.
		fàak-ngoen	*săwng-phan*	*bàat.*
		ฝากเงิน	2,000	บาท
		deposit		baht.
		on-ngoen	*săam-phan*	*bàat.*
		โอนเงิน	3,000	บาท
		transfer		baht.

PATTERN PRACTICE 8:

■ May I have your passport too?
I'd like to open an account as well.

Khǎw	*nǎng-sǔe-doen-thaang*	*dûay.*
ขอ	หนังสือเดินทาง	ด้วย
May I have...?	passport	too, as well.
	bai-à-nú-yâat-tham-ngaan	
	ใบอนุญาตทำงาน	
I'd like	work permit	
	pòet-ban-chii	
	เปิดบัญชี	
	open an account	

PATTERN PRACTICE 9:

■ Is it savings or cheque account?

Ban-chii-awm-sáp	*rǔe*	*krà-sǎe-raay-wan?*
บัญชีออมทรัพย์	หรือ	กระแสรายวัน
Savings account	or	cheque account?

PATTERN PRACTICE 10:

■ Please could you fill in the form.

Chûay	*khǐan*	*bàep-fawm*	*dûay.*
ช่วย	เขียน	แบบฟอร์ม	ด้วย
Please	fill in	account application	too.
	(lit: write)	form	

Grammar Corner

✪ **Also, too, as well**

The word *dûay,* meaning "also," "too," "as well," "in addition," is usually put at the end of a sentence or clause.

Examples:

Chăn/phŏm khăw pòet-ban-chii dûay. ฉัน/ผม ขอ เปิดบัญชี ด้วย	I'd like to open an account too.
Khun jà thăwn-ngoen dûay mái? คุณ จะ ถอนเงิน ด้วย ไหม	Would you like to withdraw some cash as well?

Exercises

EXERCISE 3: *Listen and repeat*

Khun jà lâek-ngoen thâo-rài?
คุณ จะ แลกเงิน เท่าไร

How much do you want to exchange?

Chăn/phŏm khăw lâek-ngoen nùeng-rói dawn-lâa.
ฉัน/ผม ขอ แลกเงิน 100 ดอลล่าร์

I'd like to exchange 100 U.S. dollars.

Khăw năng-sŭe-doen-thaang dûay?
ขอ หนังสือเดินทาง ด้วย

May I have your passport too?

Ban-chii-awm-sáp rŭe krà-săe-raay-wan?
บัญชีออมทรัพย์หรือกระแสรายวัน

Is it savings or cheque account?

Chûay khĭan bàep-fawm dûay.
ช่วย เขียน แบบฟอร์ม ด้วย

Please could you fill in the form.

Mii tôu-e-thii-em mái? มี ตู้เอทีเอ็ม ไหม	Is there an ATM machine around here?
Mii khâ/khráp. มี ค่ะ/ครับ	Yes, there is.
Mâi-mii khâ/khráp. ไม่มี ค่ะ/ครับ	No, there isn't.

EXERCISE 4: Write these sentences in Thai.

1. I'd like to transfer 1,500 baht.

_____

2. How much do you want to deposit?

_____

3. I would like to open an account as well.

_____

4. I'd like to withdraw some cash too.

_____

5. Please could you fill in the form.

_____

6. May I have your work permit?

_____

EXERCISE 5: Match the requests with the correct answers.

1) *Khun jà fàak-ngoen thâo-rài?*
   คุณ จะ ฝากเงิน เท่าไร

   a) *Ban-chii-awm-sáp rŭe krà-săe-raay-wan.*
   บัญชีออมทรัพย์ หรือ กระแสรายวัน

2) *Phŏm khăw pòet-ban-chii dûay.*
   ผม ขอ เปิดบัญชี ด้วย

   b) *Mii khâ.*
   มี ค่ะ

3) *Mii tôu-e-thii-em mái?*
   มี ตู้เอทีเอ็ม ไหม

   c) *Khăw năng-sŭe-doen-thaang dûay.*
   ขอ หนังสือเดินทาง ด้วย

4) *Chăn khăw thăwn-ngoen săwng-phan bàat?*
   ฉัน ขอ ถอนเงิน 2,000 บาท

   d) *Chăn khăw fàak-ngoen nùeng- phan bàat.*
   ฉัน ขอ ฝากเงิน 1,000 บาท

Cultural Notes

✪ **Mobile phone**

- It is very easy and inexpensive to buy a basic mobile phone with a Thai SIM card at any phone shop in any shopping mall. If you have your own mobile phone, you can buy a SIM card at any convenience store. You can also get top-up cards of 50, 100, 200, and 300 baht. These credits can be used for calling and sending text messages (including international calls, but read the dialing instructions carefully). You can also apply your credit to an "Internet Package" which allows you to browse the Internet wherever you are in Thailand.

- If you want to use your own phone, bear in mind that most cell phones from the US are locked and cannot be used on other networks. If you want to use a US phone with a Thai SIM card, you need to make sure that it is unlocked. Most European mobile phones will work in Thailand without any hassle. However, you are advised to check with your cell phone company before you depart to avoid any unpleasant surprises.

○ Internet access

Internet is readily available in major cities in Thailand, but still not that common in remote rural areas. Many hotels offer in-room wireless services free of charge. It is becoming increasingly common to get free Wi-Fi in cafés, restaurants, and hotel lobbies. You can also find a lot of cybercafés or Internet cafes, especially in tourist areas. They offer cheap Internet access at hourly rates, and usually serve snacks, drinks, and coffee as well.

○ Money

The baht (THB) and the satang are the currency of Thailand. The satang is a monetary unit worth one hundredth of a baht. Coins come in denominations of: 1, 2, 5 and 10 baht, as well as 25 and 50 satang. (You may get some 25 or 50 satang coins in your change at a convenience store or supermarket.) Banknotes come in denominations of: 20, 50, 100, 500, and 1,000 baht.

- ATM machines can be found all over Thailand from major cities to small towns. If your bank is a member of banking networks like Cirrus or PLUS, you should not have a problem using your ATM card in Thailand. It is definitely a good idea to inform your bank that you'll be traveling and using your ATM in Thailand before you leave your country.

○ Opening a bank account in Thailand

Whether you are only visiting Thailand for a relatively short period of time or staying for a longer time, you can open a savings account and get a debit card (ATM card) to use for shopping and ATM withdrawals. The application can be easy or difficult according to the bank, branch, or type of account needed. Each bank or each branch office may have different rules or requirements for opening an account, but general guidelines are as follows:

- If you hold a tourist visa or non-immigrant visa, all you will need to provide is your passport with a valid visa and also one other official identification document—for example, your driver's license or a reference letter from your embassy, your home bank, or a person acceptable to the bank. This is often sufficient to open the account, particularly if it's a savings account.

- If you are working in Thailand and hold a non-immigrant B visa, you will need to provide your passport showing the valid visa, and a valid work permit.

- If you are a permanent resident, or hold a long-stay visa, you can apply for a wider range of services, such as a cheque account, Internet banking, and online international funds transfer services. In this case, you will be asked to provide your valid passport together with a valid work permit and a certificate of residency from the immigration office.

Answer key

Lesson 1, Exercise 1: 1a; 2a; 3b; 4b; 5b; 6b.

Lesson 2, Exercise 2:

16 pork; 8 egg; 15 rice; 1 water; 7 chicken; 9 fish; 2 vegetables; 13 fruit; 12 deep-fry; 6 grill; 10 cook; 11 steam; 5 eat; 14 hungry; 3 yummy; 4 boil.

Lesson 3, Exercise 3:

Chǎn chûe Ann. Chǎn mii phîi-náwng sǎam khon. Chǎn mii phîi-chaay kàp náwng-chaay chǎn aa-yú sìp-kâo pii. Phîi-chaay kàp náwng-chaay khǎwng-chǎn aa-yú yîi-sìp-hâa pii kàp sìp-hòk pii. Phâw khǎwng-chǎn pen tam-rùat. Mâe khǎwng-chǎn pen phá-yaa-baan.

Lesson 4, Exercise 1:

3pm, *bàay-sǎam-mong*; 10pm, *sìi-thûm*; 5pm, *hâa-mong-yen*; 1am, *tii-nùeng*; 2pm, *bàay-sǎwng-mong*; 11am, *sìp-èt-mong-cháo*; 6pm, *hòk-mong-yen*; midnight, *thîang-khuen*; 8pm *sǎwng–thûm*; 4am, *tii-sìi*; 7pm, *nùeng-thûm*; 9am, *kâo-mong-cháo*.

Lesson 4, Exercise 2:

1. *tii-sǎam sìp naa-thii*	(3 am)
2. *nùeng-thûm*	(7 pm)
3. *kâo-mong-cháo*	(9 am)
4. *sǎam-thûm*	(9 pm)
5. *hâa-mong-yen*	(5 pm)
6. *thîang-khuen-krûeng*	(12:30 pm)
7. *bàay-sǎwng-mong hâa naa-thii*	(2:05 pm)
8. *hâa-thûm yîi-sìp naa-thii*	(11:20 pm)

Lesson 6, Exercise 2:

1) a tube of toothpaste; 2) 4 pairs of green shoes; 3) 4 pairs of socks; 4) a tooth-brush; 5) 2 yellow skirts; 6) 3 purses; 7) 2 shirts; 8) a bottle of shampoo; 9) 2 pairs of pink pants; 10) 3 pens.

Lesson 6, Exercise 3: 1b; 2a; 3b; 4b.

Lesson 7, Exercise 2:

1. *ráan-khǎay-yaa* 2. *prai-sà-nii* 3. *ráan-nǎng-sǔe* 4. *thá-na-khaan* 5. *ráan-aa-hǎan* 6. *rong-nǎng*

Lesson 7, Exercise 3:

A: *Rong-năng pai yang-ngai khá/khráp?*
B: *Nâng rót-sŏng-thăew săay yîi-sìp-pàet láew-kâw long thîi má-hăa-wít-thá-yaa-lai.*
Láew-kâw doen-trong-pai láew-kâw líaw-khwăa thîi sà-thăa-nii-tam-rùat. Rong-năng yòu trong-khâam ráan-khăay-yaa khâ/khráp.

Lesson 8, Exercise 2

1. *Wan-nii khun pen-yang-ngai bang khá?* How are you today?
2. *Rian phaa-saa-thai pen-yang-ngai baang khá?* How is Thai class?
3. *Khun sia-jai mai khá?* Are you sad?
4. *Khun sa-baay-dii rue-plao khá?* Are you all right?
5. *Khun buea rue-plao khá?* Are you bored?

Lesson 8, Exercise 3:

1. *Khun sà-baay-dii mái khá/ khráp?* 2. *Rian phaa-săa-thai sà-nùk. Chăn/phŏm tùen-tên kàp dii-jai khâ/khráp.* 3. *Náwng- săow khăwng-chăn/khăwng phŏm mâi aay loei khâ/ khráp.* 4. *Wan-níi chăn/phŏm bùea khâ/khráp.* 5. *Khun năow mái khá/ khráp?*

Lesson 9, Exercise 2:

1. A: *Khun pai-hăa-măw rúe-yang khá/ khráp?*
   B: *Chăn/phŏm pai-hăa-măw láew khâ/khráp.*
2. A: *Khun pen-yang-ngai bâang khá/ khráp?* B: *Chăn/phŏm mâi sà-baay khâ/khráp.*
3. A: *Chăn/phŏm pùat-hŭa khâ/khráp.* B: *Khun tâwng phák-phàwn khâ/khráp.*
4. A: *Khun pen à-rai khá/ khráp?* B: *Chăn/phŏm pen-wàt khâ/khráp.*
5. A: *Khun kin-yaa rúe-yang khá/ khráp?*
   B: *Chăn/phŏm yang- mâi-dâi kin-yaa khâ/khráp.*

Lesson 11, Exercise 2:

1. Jim: *Han-lŏ. Khăw phôut kàp Khun Kaew khráp.*
   Receptionist: *Khun Kaew mâi-yòu khâ.*
2. Jim: *Khun mii boe mue-thŭe Khun Sak mái khráp?*
   Receptionist: *Mii khâ.*
3. Receptionist: *Khun jà fàk-khăw-khwaam mái khá?*
   Jim: *Chûay bàwk khăo wâa phŏm tho-maa khráp.*

Lesson 11, Exercise 4:

1. *Chăn/phŏm khăw on-ngoen nùeng-phan-hâa-rôi bàat khâ/khráp.* 2. *Khun jà fàak-ngoen thâo-rài khá/khráp?* 3. *Chăn/phŏm khăw pòet-ban-chii dûay khâ/khráp.* 4. *Chăn/phŏm khăw thăwn-ngoen dûay khâ/khráp.* 5. *Chûay khĭan bàep-fawm dûay khâ/ khráp.* 6. *Khăw bai-à-nú-yâat-tham-ngaan khâ/khráp.*

Lsson 11, Exercise 5: 1d; 2a; 3b; 4c.

Thai–English Glossary

A

aa อา aunt or uncle

aa-chîip อาชีพ occupation, career

aa-hǎan อาหาร food

aa-jaan อาจารย์ teacher

aa-jian อาเจียน to vomit

aa-kàat อากาศ weather, air

àan อ่าน to read

àap-nám อาบน้ำ to take a bath, shower

aa-rom อารมณ์ emotion, mood, temper

aa-thít อาทิตย์ a week

aa-thít-nâa อาทิตย์หน้า next week

aa-thít-níi อาทิตย์นี้ this week

aa-thít-thîi-láew อาทิตย์ที่แล้ว last week

àat-jà อาจจะ could, might, may; perhaps, maybe, possibly

àaw อ่าว bay

aay อาย to be shy, embarrassed

aa-yú อายุ age

ai ไอ to cough

à-khá-tì อคติ bias, prejudice

à-me-rí-kaa อเมริกา America

am-phoe อำเภอ an administrative district

à-na-khót อนาคต the future

ang-krìt อังกฤษ England, English

à-ngùn องุ่น grapes

à-nú-yâat อนุญาต to let, allow, permit

ao เอา to take

ao-jai เอาใจ to please someone

ao-maa เอามา to bring

ao-prìap เอาเปรียบ to exploit (someone)

à-rai อะไร what

à-ròi อร่อย to be delicious, tasty

à-thí-baay อธิบาย to explain

àwk ออก out

àwk-jàak ออกจาก to leave, depart

àwn อ่อน soft, tender, mild

àwn-ae อ่อนแอ to be weak

B

bâa บ้า to be insane, crazy

bâan บ้าน home, house

baang บาง to be thin (of objects)

bâang บ้าง some, partly, somewhat

baang-thii บางที sometimes, at times

bâan-nâwk บ้านนอก countryside, rural

bàap บาป sin

bàat บาด to cut, slice, wound

bàat บาท baht

bàat-jèp บาดเจ็บ to be hurt, injured

bàay บ่าย afternoon, from midday to 4 pm

baen แบน flat

bàeng แบ่ง to divide, to share, to separate

bàep แบบ design, style, kind, pattern

bai-khàp-khìi ใบขับขี่ a driver's license

bai-mái ใบไม้ a leaf

bai-sàng-yaa ใบสั่งยา a prescription

bai-sèt ใบเสร็จ a receipt

bà-mìi บะหมี่ egg noodles

ban-chii บัญชี an account

ban-dai บันได steps, stairs, a ladder

ban-dai-lûean บันได เลื่อน an escalator

bang-kháp บังคับ to force, to compel

bang-oen บังเอิญ accidentally

ban-jù บรรจุ to load (up), to pack

ban-thúek บันทึก a note, to note

ban-yaa-kàat บรรยากาศ climate, atmosphere, ambience

ban-yaay บรรยาย to lecture, to describe

bao เบา to be light (not heavy)

bao-wǎan เบาหวาน diabetes

bàt บัตร a card, a ticket, a coupon

bàwk บอก to tell

baw-rí-jàak บริจาค to donate, give to charity

baw-rí-kaan บริการ a service, to give service

baw-rí-sàt บริษัท a company, a firm

baw-rí-wen บริเวณ a vicinity, an area

bèt เบ็ด a fish hook

bin บิน to fly

bòek เบิก to withdraw (money)

bòi บ่อย often

bon บน on, at

bòn บ่น to complain

bo-raan โบราณ ancient, old-fashioned

bòt-rian บทเรียน a lesson

bòut บูด to be rancid

bùak บวก to add on, plus

buam บวม to be swollen

bùea เบื่อ to be bored, to be tired of

bueng บึง a swamp

bù-rìi บุหรี่ cigarette

Ch

chaa ชา tea, to be numb

cháa ช้า to be slow

chaam ชาม a bowl

cháang ช้าง elephant

châang-tàt-phǒm ช่าง ตัดผม barber

châat ชาติ nation

chaaw-bâan ชาวบ้าน villager (s)

chaaw-naa ชาวนา a farmer

chaaw-tàang-châat ชาว ต่างชาติ foreigner

chaay ชาย male

chaay-hàat ชายหาด beach

chái ใช้ to use, utilize

châi ใช่ yes

chák-chuan ชักชวน to invite

chà-làat ฉลาด smart

chà-lǎwng ฉลอง to celebrate

chám ช้ำ to be bruised

chǎn ฉัน I, me

chán ชั้น a layer, level, story (of a building); class, category

chá-ná ชนะ to win, to beat, defeat

châng ชั่ง to weigh (something)

chá-nít ชนิด type, sort

châo เช่า to hire, rent

cháo เช้า morning

chát ชัด to be clear

cháwn ช้อน spoon

châwp ชอบ to be fond of; like, be pleased by

chét เช็ด to wipe

chii-wít ชีวิต life

chim ชิม to taste

chin ชิน to be accustomed (to), used to

choen เชิญ to invite (formally)

chôk โชค luck

chom ชม to admire, compliment, praise

chon-ná-bòt ชนบท rural area

chót-choey ชดเชย to compensate

chûa ชั่ว to be bad, evil

chûa-khraaw ชั่วคราว to be temporary

chûa-mong ชั่วโมง an hour, classifier for counting hours

chûay ช่วย to assist, help

chûe ชื่อ name

chûea เชื่อ to believe

chûea-fang เชื่อฟัง to obey

chúea-rôk เชื้อโรค germs

chûe-lên ชื่อเล่น nick-name

chúen ชื้น damp, humid

chùk-chŏen ฉุกเฉิน emergency

chút-nawn ชุดนอน nightclothes, pajamas

chút-wâi-nám ชุดว่ายน้ำ swimsuit

D

dàa ด่า to scold, curse

dâan ด้าน side

dâan-lăng ด้านหลัง behind

dâan-nâa ด้านหน้า front, in the front

dâan-nâwk ด้านนอก outside

daaw ดาว star

daeng แดง red

dàet แดด sunlight

dâi ได้ to get, be able to, can; get to, gain

dâi-yin ได้ยิน to hear

dam ดำ black

dam-nám ดำน้ำ to dive

dan ดัน to push, shove

dang ดัง to be loud (sound), to be famous

dao เดา to guess

dàwk-mái ดอกไม้ flower

dèk เด็ก child

dèk-phôu-chaay เด็กผู้ชาย boy

dèk-phôu-yĭng เด็กผู้หญิง girl

diaw เดียว single, one, only

dĭaw เดี๋ยว for a moment, just a moment

dĭaw-níi เดี๋ยวนี้ right now, now

dì-chăn ดิฉัน I, me (female, formal)

dii ดี good, nice, well

dii-jai ดีใจ glad, happy

din ดิน earth, soil, ground

din-săw ดินสอ pencil

dìp ดิบ raw, uncooked, unripe

doen เดิน to walk

doen-lên เดินเล่น to go for a walk

doen-thaang เดินทาง to travel, take a trip

dom ดม to smell, inhale, sniff

don-trii ดนตรี music

dou ดู to look at, to see, to watch (TV, movie)

dou-lae ดูแล to take care of, look after

dòut ดูด to suck, to absorb, soak up

dou-thòuk ดูถูก to look down on someone, insult

dùan ด่วน to be urgent

duang-jan ดวงจันทร์ moon

dûay ด้วย also, too

dûe ดื้อ stubborn

duean เดือน month

dùeat-ráwn เดือดร้อน to be in trouble

dùek ดึก late at night

dùem ดื่ม to drink

dueng ดึง to pull

E

èk-kà-săan เอกสาร document(s)

eo เอว waist

F

fǎa ฝา lid, cover

fáa ฟ้า light blue, sky

fàak-ngoen ฝากเงิน to deposit money

fáa-phàa ฟ้าผ่า lightning

fǎa-phà-nǎng ฝาผนัง wall (of a room or building)

fáa-ráwng ฟ้าร้อง thunder

fâay ฝ้าย cotton

faen แฟน boy/girlfriend, fan (admirer)

fai ไฟ fire; light (lamp)

fǎi ไฝ mole, beauty spot

fai-fáa ไฟฟ้า electricity

fan ฟัน teeth

fǎn ฝัน dream, to dream

fawng ฟอง foam, bubbles

fáwng ฟ้อง to sue, complain to someone about somebody else

fawng-nám ฟองน้ำ a sponge

fǒn ฝน rain

fǒn-tòk ฝนตก to rain

fùek ฝึก to practice, to drill/train

fùn ฝุ่น dust

H

hâa ห้า five

hǎa หา look for, look up (in book)

hâam ห้าม to forbid, to be forbidden

hàan ห่าน goose

hǎng หาง tail

hǎaw หาว to yawn

hǎay หาย lost, disappear, to be missing

hǎa-yâak หายาก rare

hǎay-jai หายใจ to breathe

hâeng แห้ง to be dry

hâi-yuem ให้ยืม to lend

hàk หัก to break (bones), to deduct (money owed, etc.)

hàn หั่น to cut up, slice

hǎn หัน to turn

hǎn-nâa หันหน้า to face, turn one's head,

hào เห่า to bark

hàw ห่อ to wrap

hǎwm หอม to be sweet-smelling,

hâwng ห้อง room

hâwng-khrua ห้องครัว kitchen

hâwng-náam ห้องน้ำ lavatory

hâwng-nâng-lên ห้องนั่งเล่น sitting room, living room

hâwng-nawn ห้องนอน bedroom

hâwng-sà-mùt ห้องสมุด library

hǎw-phák หอพัก dormitory

hěn เห็น to see

hěn-dûay เห็นด้วย to agree

hěn-jai เห็นใจ to be sympathetic

hěn-kàe-tua เห็นแก่ตัว to be selfish

hèt เห็ด mushroom(s)

hèt-phǒn เหตุผล reason

hì-má หิมะ snow

hǐn หิน rock, stone

hǐw หิว to be hungry

hîw หิ้ว to carry

hǐw-náam หิวน้ำ to be thirsty

hòk หก six, to spill (liquid)

hǒng หงส์ a swan

hòt หด to shrink

hǒu หู ear(s)

hǒu-nùak หูหนวก to be deaf

hǒi หอย shellfish

hôi ห้อย to hang

hǒi-naang-rom หอยนางรม a type of large, fleshy oyster

hǒi-thâak หอยทาก snail

hǔa หัว head, top

hǔa-bo-raan หัวโบราณ to be old fashioned, conservative

hǔa-jai-waay หัวใจวาย a heart attack

hǔa-khǎeng หัวแข็ง obstinate, stubborn

hǔa-khào หัวเข่า knee

hǔa-láan หัวล้าน bald

hǔa-mum หัวมุม corner

hǔa-nâa หัวหน้า chief, leader, head, boss

hǔang หวง to be jealous (of), possessive (of things)

hùang (adj) ห่วง anxious, worried (about)

hǔa-ráw หัวเราะ to laugh

hǔay หวย underground lottery

hùn หุ่น mannequin, also the shape of someone's figure;

hǔng หุง to cook (rice)

hùn-yon หุ่นยนต์ robot

hûn-sùan หุ้นส่วน partner (in business)

I

iik อีก again

ii-sǎan อีสาน the northeastern region of Thailand

im อิ่ม to be full, eaten one's fill, had enough

it อิฐ brick, a brick

it-chǎa อิจฉา envy, be jealous of

it-sà-rà อิสระ to be free, independent

it-sà-rà-phâap อิสรภาพ freedom

it-thí-phon อิทธิพล influence

J

jàak จาก from

jaam จาม to sneeze

jaan จาน a plate, dish

jâang จ้าง to hire

jàay จ่าย to pay

jam-dâi จำได้ to remember, recognize

jàek แจก to hand out, distribute

jae-kan แจกัน a vase

jâeng แจ้ง to inform, to notify

jai ใจ heart, mind

jai-dam ใจดำ to be unkind, mean

jai-dii ใจดี to be kind

jai-khâep ใจแคบ to be ungenerous, narrow-minded

jai-kwâang ใจกว้าง to be generous, broad-minded

jai-loi ใจลอย lose concentration, zone out

jai-ráwn ใจร้อน impatient

jai-yen ใจเย็น calm, patient

jàk-kà-yaan จักรยาน bicycle

jam จำ to remember, to retain

jam-nuan จำนวน amount

jam-pen จำเป็น to be necessary, to need

jà-mòuk (n) จมูก nose

jang-wàt จังหวัด a province

jâo-bàaw เจ้าบ่าว bridegroom/groom

jâo-nâa-thîi เจ้าหน้าที่ official, bureaucrat

jâo-phâap เจ้าภาพ a host (of a party, etc.)

jâo-sǎaw เจ้าสาว bride

jàp จับ to capture, arrest, catch

jà-raa-jawn จราจร traffic

jàt จัด to arrange

jaw จอ screen, monitor (of TV/computer)

jawng จอง to reserve, to book (seats, tickets)

jàwt-rót จอดรถ to park a vehicle

je เจ (Chinese) vegetarian

jèp เจ็บ to be sore, hurt (injured)

jèp-khaw เจ็บคอ a sore throat

jèp-taa เจ็บตา sore eyes

jiin จีน China, Chinese

jiip จีบ to flirt with someone, to court

jing จริง to be true, real

jing-jô จิงโจ้ kangaroo

jîng-jòk จิ้งจก house lizard

jîng-rìit จิ้งหรีด cricket (insect)

joe เจอ to meet, find

jom จม to sink, drown

jon จน to be poor

jon-krà-thâng จนกระทั่ง until

jòp จบ to end (finish)

jòt จด to take note

jòt-mǎay จดหมาย letter; mail

jòup จูบ kiss

jùeng จึง so, therefore

jùet จืด bland, tasteless

jùt จุด point, dot

jùt-fai จุดไฟ to light a fire

K

kaa-fae กาแฟ coffee

kâang ก้าง fishbone

kaang-keng กางเกง trousers, pants

kaang-keng-khǎa-sân กางเกงขาสั้น shorts, short pants

kaang-keng-khǎa-yaaw กางเกงขายาว long pants, trousers

kaang-keng-nai กางเกงใน underpants, panties

kaang-keng-yiin กางเกงยีน jeans

kaan-khàeng-khǎn การแข่งขัน competition, race

kaan-lûeak-tâng การเลือกตั้ง election

kaan-mueang การเมือง politics

kaan-ngoen การเงิน finance

kaan-phát-thá-naa การพัฒนา development

kaan-sà-daeng การแสดง a display, a show, a performance

kaan-sùek-sǎa การศึกษา education

kaaw กาว glue

kâaw ก้าว step

kâaw-nâa ก้าวหน้า to advance, go forward

kàe แกะ sheep

kàe แก่ old (person), strong (coffee)

kâe แก้ to fix (repair), to loosen, to correct

kâem แก้ม cheek(s)

kaeng แกง soup/curry dish

kaeng-jùet แกงจืด clear soup

kaeng-phèt แกงเผ็ด spicy curry

kâe-pan-hǎa แก้ปัญหา to solve (a problem)

kàe-sà-làk แกะสลัก to carve

kâe-tua แก้ตัว to make excuses, find an excuse

kâew แก้ว glass (for drinking)

kài ไก่ chicken

kài-thâwt ไก่ทอด fried chicken

kài-yâang ไก่ย่าง grilled chicken

kà-làm-dàwk กะหล่ำดอก cauliflower

kà-làm-plii กะหล่ำปลี cabbage

kam กรรม karma

kam-jàt กำจัด to rid, get rid of

kam-lang กำลัง strength, power, (armed) force

kam-nan กำนัน subdistrict headman, chief of sub-district

kam-phaeng กำแพง (stone or brick) wall (of a yard or town)

kam-rai กำไร profit

kan กัน each other

kan-khrai กรรไกร scissors

kan-yaa-yon กันยายน September

kao เกา to scratch lightly

kào เก่า old (of things)

kâo-îi เก้าอี้ chair

kàp กับ with, and

kà-pì กะปิ fish paste

kà-phrao กะเพรา sweet basil

kà-rá-kà-daa-khom กรกฎาคม July

kà-rú-naa กรุณา please (formal)

kà-sèt-trà-kawn เกษตรกร farmer

kàt กัด to bite

kà-thí กะทิ coconut cream/milk

kà-thoei กะเทย a transvestite, ladyboy

kàw เกาะ island

kàwn ก่อน first, earlier, before

kawng-tháp กองทัพ troops, the military, the army (in particular)

kàwt กอด to embrace

kàw-tâng ก่อตั้ง to establish, set up

ké เก๊ fake

kè เก๋ to be stylish, chic

kèng เก่ง clever, smart, good at something

kèp เก็บ to save, keep, pick up

kèp-khǎwng เก็บของ to gather things together, to pack

kèp-tó เก็บโต๊ะ to clear the table

kèp-tua เก็บตัว to avoid others, to keep to oneself, to shun society

kìat เกียรติ honour, dignity

kìaw-kàp เกี่ยวกับ about, regarding

kìaw-khâwng เกี่ยวข้อง to involve, in connection with

kìi กี่ how many?

kii-laa กีฬา sport(s)

kìit-khwǎang กีดขวาง to hinder, obstruct

kin กิน to eat, (slang) to be corrupt, take bribes

kìng-mái กิ่งไม้ the branch of a tree

kit-jà-kam กิจกรรม activity

klâa-hǎan กล้าหาญ to be brave, daring

klâam-núea กล้ามเนื้อ muscle(s)

klaang กลาง in the middle, center

klaang-khuen กลางคืน night

klaang-mueang กลางเมือง city/ town center

klaang-wan กลางวัน day, daytime

klaay-pen กลายเป็น to become

klâeng แกล้ง to pretend, to tease someone (maliciously), to annoy (deliberately)

klâi ใกล้ near, close to

klai ไกล to be far away, distant, a long way

klàp กลับ to return (home), to turn over

klàp-bâan กลับบ้าน to return home

klàp-jai กลับใจ to have a change of heart, to be reformed

klawng กลอง a drum

klâwng กล้อง a camera; also pipe

klàwng กล่อง box

klàwng-kra-dàat กล่อง กระดาษ cardboard box

klìat เกลียด to hate

klìn กลิ่น odor, smell

klom กลม round (shape)

klua กลัว to fear

klûay กล้วย banana

klûay-mái กล้วยไม้ orchid(s)

kluea เกลือ salt

kluen กลืน to swallow

klùm กลุ่ม group

klûm-jai กลุ่มใจ to be depressed, glum

koen เกิน to exceed

kòet เกิด to be born

kòet-khuen เกิดขึ้น to happen

kôm ก้ม to bend down, stoop, bow

kon โกน to shave

kôn ก้น bottom, buttocks

kong โกง to cheat

kòp กบ a frog

kòt กฎ rule, law

kòt กด to press

kòt-mǎay กฎหมาย laws, legislation

kôu กู้ to borrow (money), take a loan

kôy ก้อย little finger, pinky

kraam กราม jaw

kràap กราบ to prostrate oneself (as a sign of respect), (in some contexts) to grovel

krà-daan กระดาน board, plank

krà-dàat กระดาษ paper

krà-dàat-khǎeng กระดาษแข็ง cardboard

krà-dòt กระโดด to jump

krà-dòuk กระดูก bone(s)

krà-dòuk-sǎn-lǎng กระดูกสันหลัง the spine, backbone

krà-jaay-sǐang กระจายเสียง to broadcast

krà-jòk กระจก glass (material), the windshield of a car, a mirror

krà-pǎo กระเป๋า a bag, garment pocket

krà-pǎo-doen-thaang กระเป๋าเดินทาง a suitcase

krà-pǎo-ngoen กระเป๋าเงิน wallet

krà-pǎo-tham-ngaan กระเป๋าทำงาน briefcase

krà-pǎwng กระป๋อง a can, tin

krà-prong กระโปรง a skirt

krà-síp กระซิบ to whisper

krà-suang กระทรวง (government) ministry

krà-sǔn กระสุน a bullet

krà-tàay กระต่าย rabbit

krà-thá กระทะ a wok

krà-thâwm กระท่อม hut, shack, cottage

krà-thiam กระเทียม garlic

krà-tik กระติก ice cooler

krawng กรอง to filter

kràwp กรอบ crisp, brittle

kràwp กรอบ a frame, (within the) confines/ limitations (of)

kràwp-rôup กรอบรูป a (picture) frame

kreng เกร็ง tense, stiffened, to flex a muscle

kreng-jai เกรงใจ A key Thai concept which means a fear of imposing on someone else, considerate

krom กรม (a government) department

kron กรน to snore

krong กรง cage

kròt โกรธ to be upset

kuan กวน to bother, annoy, disturb

kǔay-tǐaw ก๋วยเตี๋ยว noodles

kùeap เกือบ almost, nearly

kù-làap กุหลาบ a rose (bush/flower)

kum-phaa-phan กุมภาพันธ์ February

kûng กุ้ง shrimp, prawn

kun-jae กุญแจ key (to room)

kun-jae-mue กุญแจมือ handcuffs

kwâang กว้าง broad, spacious, wide

kwàat กวาด to sweep

kwàeng แกว่ง to swing

Kh

khá คะ polite question ending (for women)

khâ ค่ะ polite statement ending (for women)

khàa ข่า galangal

khǎa ขา leg(s)

khâa ค่า value (cost)

khâa ฆ่า kill, murder

khâa-chái-jàay ค่าใช้จ่าย expenses

khâa-doy-sǎan ค่าโดยสาร fare (for a bus, plane trip)

khâa-jâang ค่าจ้าง wage(s)

khâam ข้าม across, cross, go over

khan ค้าน to oppose, be opposed to

khâang ข้าง side

kháang-khuen ค้างคืน to stay overnight

khâa-pràp ค่าปรับ a fine (for an infringement)

khàat ขาด to lack, lack of, to be lacking, to be insufficient, to be torn, to break (e.g. a rope)

khǎaw ขาว white

khàaw ข่าว news, report

khâaw ข้าว rice

khàaw-lue ข่าวลือ rumor

khâaw-nǐaw ข้าวเหนียว sticky rice

khâaw-phàt ข้าวผัด fried rice

khâaw-phôt ข้าวโพด corn

khâaw-sǔay ข้าวสวย steamed rice

khâaw-tôm ข้าวต้ม boiled rice

khǎay ขาย for sale, to sell

khàek แขก guest

khǎen แขน arm(s)

khàeng แข่ง to compete against in a race

khǎeng แข็ง to be hard (not soft)

khǎeng-raeng แข็งแรง to be strong

khâep แคบ narrow

khài ไข่ egg

khâi ไข้ fever

khài-daeng ไข่แดง egg yolk

khài-khǎaw ไข่ขาว egg white

khǎi-man ไขมัน fat (body fat), grease

khâi-wàt-yài ไข้หวัด ใหญ่ flu, influenza

kham-sàp คำศัพท์ vocabulary

kham-tàwp คำตอบ answer, response

kham-thǎam คำถาม question

khà-moy ขโมย to steal, a thief, thieves

khan คัน to be itchy

khân ขั้น stage, grade, step, rank

khà-nǒm ขนม sweets, dessert, snacks

khâo เข้า to enter, go in

khâo-jai เข้าใจ to understand

khâo-jai-phìt เข้าใจผิด to misunderstand

khàp ขับ to drive

khǎw ขอ to ask for, request (informally), apply for permission, please

khaw คอ neck

khâw-khwaam ข้อความ message

khǎwng-chǎn ของฉัน my, mine (female)

khǎwng-khǎo ของเขา his/her/their

khǎwng-khun ของฉัน your, yours

khǎwng-khwǎn ของ ขวัญ a present (gift)

khǎwng-phǒm ของผม my, mine (men)

khǎwng-plawm ของ ปลอม a copy, a fake, pirated merchandise

khàwp-khun ขอบคุณ to thank, thank you

khǎw-ráwng ขอร้อง to request (formally)

khǎw-thôt ขอโทษ to apologize, sorry, excuse me

khà-yà ขยะ garbage, rubbish

khà-yǎn ขยัน to be hardworking, diligent

khěm-khàt เข็มขัด belt

khǐang เขียง a chopping board

khíaw เคี้ยว to chew

khít คิด to think, to have an opinion

khít-thǔeng คิดถึง to miss (e.g. a loved one)

khoei เคย to be used to

khoi คอย to wait for

khôu คู่ a pair of

khrai ใคร who

khràp ครับ polite ending for men

khrâwp-krua ครอบครัว family

khrou ครู teacher

khrûeang-bin เครื่อง บิน an airplane

khrûeang-dùem เครื่อง ดื่ม drink, refreshment

khrûeang-prung เครื่อง ปรุง seasoning, ingredient

khrûeng ครึ่ง half

khùat ขวด bottle

khûen ขึ้น to go up, to get on

khun คุณ you (pronoun)

khuy คุย to chat

khwǎa ขวา right (direction)

khwaam-chûea ความ เชื่อ belief, faith

khwaam-khrîat ความ เครียด tension, stress

khwaam-láp ความลับ secret, confidentiality

khwaam-mân-jai ความ มั่นใจ confidence

khwaam-phá-yaa-yaam ความพยายาม attempt, effort

khwaam-róu ความรู้ knowledge

khwaam-róu-sùek ความรู้สึก feeling, emotion

khwaam-sa-àat ความ สะอาด cleanliness

khwaam-sǎa-mâat ความสามารถ ability, capacity

L

laa-àwk ลาออก to resign, quit (a job)

láan ล้าน million

lǎan หลาน grandchild, niece, nephew

lǎan-chaay หลานชาย grandson

lǎan-sǎaw หลานสาว granddaughter

lâang ล่าง below

lǎay หลาย several

láe และ and

lâek-ngoen แลกเงิน to exchange money

lǎng หลัง back (of body)

lǎng-khaa หลังคา roof

lâo เหล้า liquor, alcohol

làw หล่อ to be handsome

lawng ลอง to try on

lâo เล่า to tell a story, relate

léb เล็บ nail

lék เล็ก small

lèk เหล็ก iron, metal

lêm เล่ม classifier for books

lên เล่น to play

leo เลว bad (of a person)

líang เลี้ยง to bring up, raise (children or animals); to treat (someone)

líaw เลี้ยว to turn

líaw-khwǎa เลี้ยวขวา to turn right

líaw-sáay เลี้ยวซ้าย to turn left

lín ลิ้น tongue

lín-chák ลิ้นชัก drawer

loei เลย really, indeed

lôek เลิก to cease, stop, give up (e.g. smoking cigarettes)

loi ลอย to float

lôk โลก the earth, world

lom ลม wind, breeze

lóm ล้ม to topple, fall over, collapse, to overthrow (a government)

long ลง to go down, get off

lòp หลบ to avoid, evade, duck, shy away

lót ลด to reduce, discount

lôuk ลูก child (offspring)

lôuk-chaay ลูกชาย son

lôuk-kháa ลูกค้า customer, client

lôuk-phîi-lôuk-náwng ลูกพี่ลูกน้อง cousin

lôuk-sǎaw ลูกสาว daughter

lǔam หลวม loose (the opposite of tight)

lûeak เลือก to choose

lûean เลื่อน to put off, delay

lǔeang เหลือง yellow

lûeat เลือด blood

lúek ลึก deep (e.g. water), profound

lúek-láp ลึกลับ to be mysterious

luem ลืม to forget

lûen ลื่น to slip, to be slippery

lúk ลุก to stand, get up, rise

M

maa มา to come

máa ม้า horse

mǎa หมา dog

maa-jàak มาจาก to come from

mâak มาก very, a lot

màak-fà-ràng หมาก ฝรั่ง chewing gum

maa-rá-yâat มารยาท behaviour, manners

mâe แม่ mother

mâe-bâan แม่บ้าน housekeeper, housewife, lady of the house

mâe-nám แม่น้ำ river

maew แมว cat

má-hǎa-sà-mùt มหาสมุทร ocean

má-hǎa-wít-thá-yaa-lai มหาวิทยาลัย university

mài ใหม่ new

mâi ไม่ no, not

mái ไม้ wood

mǎi ไหม yes-no question, silk

mâi ไหม้ to burn

mâi-châwp ไม่ชอบ to dislike

mái-jîm-fan ไม้จิ้มฟัน toothpick(s)

mái-khìit-fai ไม้ขีดไฟ matches

mâi-pen-rai ไม่เป็นไร that's alright, it doesn't matter

má-khǎam มะขาม tamarind (fruit)

má-khǔea-thêt มะเขือ เทศ tomato

má-laeng แมลง insect

má-lá-kaw มะละกอ papaya

má-mûang มะม่วง mango

má-naaw มะนาว lime

mang-khút มังคุด mangosteen

má-práaw มะพร้าว coconut

má-reng มะเร็ง cancer

mǎw หมอ doctor

màwk หมอก mist, fog

mǎwn หมอน pillow, cushion

mawng มอง to watch, to stare at

màw-sǒm เหมาะสม to be suitable

měn เหม็น to stink

me-săa-yon เมษายน April

mii มี to have, there is/ there are

mii-khâa มีค่า to be valuable, precious, to have worth/be useful

mii-khwaam-sùk มีความสุข to be happy

mii-naa-khom มีนาคม March

mii-prà-yòt มีประโยชน์ to be useful

mí-thù-naa-yon มิถุนายน June

mo-hŏ โมโห to be angry

mók-kà-raa-khom มกราคม January

mong โมง o'clock

mong-cháo โมงเช้า o'clock in the morning

mong-yen โมงเย็น o'clock in the evening

mòt-aa-yú หมดอายุ to expire

mŏu หมู pig, pork

mòu-bâan หมู่บ้าน village

mùak หมวก hat, cap

mûang ม่วง purple

muay มวย boxing

mue มือ hand

mûea เมื่อ when (conjunction)

mŭean เหมือน to resemble; like, as

mûea-rài เมื่อไร when (question), at what time?

mûea-waan-níi เมื่อ วานนี้ yesterday

mùek หมึก ink

mùen หมื่น ten thousand

mûet มืด dark

mue-thŭe มือถือ mobile phone

múk มุก pearl

múng มุ้ง mosquito net

N

naa นา rice field

nâa หน้า face, page

náa น้า aunt

nâa-bùea น่าเบื่อ boring, dull

nâa-klìat น่าเกลียด ugly (person, thing, behaviour)

nâa-klua น่ากลัว scary, frightening

naa-lí-kaa นาฬิกา watch, clock

náam น้ำ water

náam-àt-lom น้ำอัดลม soft drink, soda

náam-chaa น้ำชา tea

náam-hŏwm น้ำหอม perfume

náam-jîm น้ำจิ้ม sauce (for dipping)

náam-khăeng น้ำแข็ง ice

náam-nàk น้ำหนัก weight

náam-ngoen น้ำเงิน dark blue

náam-phŏn-lá-mái น้ำ ผลไม้ fruit juice

náam-phûeng น้ำผึ้ง honey

náam-plaa น้ำปลา fish sauce

náam-sà-kun นามสกุล last name

náam-taan น้ำตาล sugar, brown (color)

náam-tòk น้ำตก waterfall

nâa-rák น่ารัก cute

nâa-sà-nùk น่าสนุก to be fun, to look like fun

nâa-sŏn-jai น่าสนใจ interesting

nâa-taa หน้าตา look, appearance

nâa-tàang หน้าต่าง window

naa-thii นาที minute

nâa-tùen-tên น่าตื่น เต้น to be exciting

năw หนาว to be cold

nâe-jai แน่ใจ certain, sure

náe-nam แนะนำ to suggest, advise

nai ใน in

nàk หนัก to be heavy

nák-bin นักบิน a pilot, aviator

nák-ráwng นักร้อง a singer

nák-rian นักเรียน school student

nák-sùek-sǎa นักศึกษา university student

nák-thâwng-thîaw นัก ท่องเที่ยว a tourist

nân นั่น that

nâng นั่ง to sit

nǎng หนัง movie

nǎng-sǔe หนังสือ book

nǎng-sǔe-phim หนังสือพิมพ์ newspaper

nâo เน่า to be rotten, spoiled (food)

náp นับ count, reckon

nawn นอน to sleep

náwng-chaay น้องชาย younger brother

náwng-sǎaw น้องสาว younger sister

nǐaw เหนียว sticky, tough, chewy

nîi นี่ this

nǐi หนี to run away, escape, get away

ní-sǎi นิสัย habit, character

nít-nòi นิดหน่อย a bit

níw นิ้ว finger, inch

noey เนย butter

nói น้อย to be little, less, slight (in quantity)

nók นก bird

nom นม milk; breasts

nùat หนวด moustache

nûat นวด to massage

núea เนื้อ meat, flesh

nùeay เหนื่อย to be exhausted, fatigue

nùeng หนึ่ง one (number)

nûeng นึ่ง to steam

nûm นุ่ม soft

Ng

ngaa งา sesame seeds

ngaam งาม to be beautiful; fine, good

ngaan งาน work (noun)

ngaan-à-dì-rèk งาน อดิเรก hobby

ngaan-bâan งานบ้าน housework

ngaan-sòp งานศพ funeral

ngaan-tàeng-ngaan งาน แต่งงาน wedding

ngâay ง่าย to be simple, easy

ngǎo เหงา lonely

ngîap เงียบ to be quiet, silent

ngô โง่ to be stupid

ngoen เงิน money, silver

ngoen-duean เงินเดือน salary

ngoen-sòt เงินสด cash

ngong งง to be puzzled, stunned, confused

ngou งู snake

ngûang-nawn ง่วงนอน to be sleepy, tired

ngùea เหงื่อ sweat

O

o-kàat โอกาส chance, opportunity

on โอน to transfer (money)

òn อ่อน to be light (in color)

òng โอ่ง earthen jar, (large) water jar

òp อบ to bake, baked, to roast

òp-choey อบเชย cinnamon

òp-phá-yóp อพยพ to migrate, evacuate

òp-ùn อบอุ่น warm

òt อด to give up, abstain from

òt-aa-hǎan อดอาหาร to fast, go without food

òt-thon อดทน to be patient, to have tenacity, stamina

ôy อ้อย sugarcane

P

pàa ป่า forest, jungle

pàak ปาก mouth

pàak-kaa ปากกา pen

pâeng แป้ง powder, flour

pàet แปด eight

pai ไป to go

pai-klàp ไปกลับ round trip

pai-năi-maa ไปไหนมา Where have you been?

pai-thîaw ไปเที่ยว to take a trip, go out

pào เป่า to blow out (flame)

pâo-măay เป้าหมาย goal, objective

pà-tì-bàt ปฏิบัติ (formal) to operate, perform

pà-tì-sèt ปฏิเสธ to decline, refuse, deny

pâwn ป้อน to feed someone, to spoon feed

pen เป็น to be

pen-prà-jam เป็น ประจำ always

pèt เป็ด duck

pìak เปียก to be wet, soaking

pii ปี year

pii-nâa ปีหน้า next year

pii-níi ปีนี้ this year

pii-thîi-láew ปีที่แล้ว last year

pìt ปิด to close

plaa ปลา fish

plaa-mùek ปลาหมึก squid

plae แปล to translate

plàek แปลก strange, unusual, odd; a stranger

plawm ปลอม to forge, counterfeit, fake

plàwt-phai ปลอดภัย to be safe

plìan เปลี่ยน to change

plìan-jai เปลี่ยนใจ to change one's mind

plueay เปลือย to be naked, nude

pòet เปิด to open

pou ปู crab

pòu ปู่ paternal grand-father

prà-chum ประชุม to hold a meeting

praeng-fan แปรงฟัน to brush one's teeth

praeng-sĭi-fan แปรงสีฟัน tooth-brush

prai-sà-nii ไปรษณีย์ post office

prà-kàat ประกาศ to announce, declare

prà-maan ประมาณ about, approximately

prà-tháp-jai ประทับใจ to be impressed, im-pressive

prà-thêt ประเทศ country

prà-tou ประตู door

prà-wàt ประวัติ personal history, record, resumé

prà-yàt ประหยัด to economize, economi-cal, to be thrifty, frugal

prà-yòt ประโยชน์ usefulness, utility, (for the) benefit (of), advantage

prùek-săa ปรึกษา to consult with

Ph

phaa พา to take or lead someone somewhere

phâa ผ้า cloth

phâa-mâan ผ้าม่าน curtain(s), drapes

phàan ผ่าน to pass, go past; (to go) via, through

phâap ภาพ picture

phaa-săa ภาษา lan-guage

phàa-tàt ผ่าตัด to operate, to perform an operation or surgery

phaa-yú พายุ storm

phae แพ a raft, houseboat

pháe แพ้ to lose, be defeated; to be allergic

phaeng แพง expensive, dear, costly

phǎen-thîi แผนที่ map

phâi ไพ่ card game

phai ภัย danger, peril

phàk ผัก vegetable

phák-phàwn พักผ่อน to rest

phá-lang พลัง energy, power (e.g. physical energy, solar energy, wind power, etc.)

phá-lang-ngaan พลังงาน energy

phà-lìt ผลิต to manufacture, produce

phá-nák-ngaan พนักงาน employee in a department store/ large enterprise

phá-nák-ngaan-khǎay พนักงานขาย sales assistant

phá-nan พนัน gamble; to gamble

phang พัง broken down, in ruins, ruined

phan-rá-yaa ภรรยา wife (formal term)

phǎo เผา to burn

pháp พับ to fold, to double over

phà-sǒm ผสม to mix, combine

phàt ผัด to stir fry

phát-lom พัดลม electric fan

phát-thá-naa พัฒนา to develop (e.g. a project)

phaw พอ enough, sufficient

phâw พ่อ father

phaw-jai พอใจ to be satisfied, pleased

phǎwm ผอม to be skinny

phá-yaa-baan พยาบาล nurse

phá-yaa-yaam พยายาม to try, make an effort

phèt เผ็ด to be spicy

phêt เพศ gender, sex

phîi-chaay พี่ชาย older brother

phîi-náwn พี่น้อง siblings

phîi-sǎaw น้องชาย older sister

phí-sèt พิเศษ special, extra

phìt ผิด to be false, guilty, wrong

phìt-wǎng ผิดหวัง to be disappointed

phǐu ผิว skin, complexion

phlǎe แผล scar, cut, wound

phǒm ผม I (for male speaker), hair

phǒn-lá-mái ผลไม้ fruit

phóp พบ to find, meet

phôu-chaay ผู้ชาย man, male

phou-khǎo ภูเขา mountain

phoum-jai ภูมิใจ to be proud

phôu-phí-phâak-sǎa ผู้พิพากษา judge (in a court of law)

phôut พูด speak

phôu-yài ผู้ใหญ่ adult

phôu-yïng ผู้หญิง woman, female

phrá พระ (Buddhist) monk, Buddhist amulets, images

phráw เพราะ because

phrík พริก chili pepper

phrúet-sà-ji-kaa-yon พฤศจิกายน November

phrúet-sà-phaa-khom พฤษภาคม May

phrûng-níi พรุ่งนี้ tomorrow

phûea เพื่อ in order to

phûean-bâan เพื่อนบ้าน neighbor(s)

phùen ผื่น rash

phûeng ผึ้ง bee(s)

R

raa-khaa ราคา price, value, worth

ráan ร้าน shop, store, vendor's stall

ráan-aa-hǎan ร้านอาหาร restaurant

râang-kaay ร่างกาย body

raang-wan รางวัล a prize, reward

ráan-khǎay-yaa ร้านขายยา drugstore

ráan-nǎng-sǔe ร้านหนังสือ bookstore

raay-dâi รายได้ income

raay-jàay รายจ่าย expense

rá-bòp ระบบ a system

râek แรก original, first, initial

rá-hàt รหัส password, code

rái-sǎa-rá ไร้สาระ nonsense

rák รัก to love, be fond of

rák-sǎa รักษา to cure

ram-khaan รำคาญ to be annoyed, irritated

rang-kìat รังเกียจ to mind, dislike

rao เรา we (pronoun)

ráp รับ to receive; to get, pick someone up

ráp-sǎay รับสาย to answer the phone

rát รัฐ state

rát-thà-baan รัฐบาล government

raw รอ to wait (for, at, in, on)

rá-wàang ระหว่าง between

rá-wang ระวัง to be careful, watch out

ráwn ร้อน to be hot

ráwng-hâi ร้องไห้ to cry, weep

ráwng-pleng ร้องเพลง to sing

rawng-thóa รองเท้า shoes

rá-yá-thaang ระยะทาง distance (e.g. of a journey)

rêng เร่ง to hurry, accelerate

rîak เรียก to call, demand, summon

rian เรียน to study

rîap-rói เรียบร้อย to be neat

rîip รีบ to hurry, rush

rôem เริ่ม to start

rói ร้อย hundred

rôm ร่ม shade, umbrella **rong-nǎng** โรงหนัง movie theater

rong-phá-yaa-baan โรงพยาบาล hospital

rong-raem โรงแรม hotel

rong-rian โรงเรียน school

róp-kuan รบกวน to bother, disturb

rót รถ car (wheeled vehicles in general)

rót รส flavour, taste

rót รด to water (plants)

rót-fai รถไฟ train

rót-náam รดน้ำ to water plants/garden

rót-tìt รถติด traffic jam

róu รู้ to know, realize

róu-jàk รู้จัก to know a person/a place, be acquainted with

rôup รูป photo

rǒu-rǎa หรูหรา luxurious

róu-sùek รู้สึก to feel, sense, have a feeling (of, that)

róu-sùek-phìt รู้สึกผิด to feel guilty

rúa รั้ว a fence

rûa รั่ว to leak

ruay รวย to be rich, well off, wealthy

rǔe หรือ or

ruea เรือ boat, ship

rûeang เรื่อง story, subject, about

rúe-dou ฤดู (formal term) season

rúe-dou-bai-mái-phlì ฤดูใบไม้ผลิ spring (season)

rúe-dou-bai-mái-rûang ฤดูใบไม้ร่วง autumn/fall

rúe-dou-fǒn ฤดูฝน rainy season (formal)

rúe-dou-nǎo ฤดูหนาว cool season (formal), winter

rúe-dou-ráwn ฤดูร้อน hot season (formal), summer

rúe-plào หรือเปล่า Are you...? Is it...?

S

sà-àat สะอาด to be clean

sǎa-hèt สาเหตุ cause, reason (for)

sǎa-mii สามี husband

sǎan ศาล court (of law)

sâang สร้าง to build, construct, create

sâap-súeng ซาบซึ้ง to appreciate, to be grateful (for), heartfelt

sàat-sà-nǎa ศาสนา religion

sáay ซ้าย left

sǎay สาย to be late; number of bus

sǎay-mâi-wâang สาย ไม่ว่าง the line is busy

sà-baay สบาย to be comfortable

sà-baay-dii สบายดี to be fine

sà-baay-jai สบายใจ to be happy

sà-bòu สบ่ soap

sài ใส่ to add, to put on

sǎm-khan สำคัญ important, significant

sǎm-rèt สำเร็จ to be finished, completed, accomplished, successful, (v) to succeed;

sà-mùt สมุด notebook

sà-mùt-ban-chii สมุด บัญชี bank account book

sân สั้น to be short

sà-nǎam-bin สนามบิน airport

sà-nè เสน่ห์ charm, attraction, appeal

sǎng-khom สังคม society

sà-ngòp สงบ peaceful, calm

sà-nùk สนุก fun, enjoyable, entertaining, to have a good time

sǎn-yaa สัญญา to promise; a contract

sâo เศร้า sad

sà-phaan สะพาน bridge

sà-phǒm สระผม to wash hair

sàp-pà-rót สับปะรด pineapple

sàp-sǒn สับสน to be confused, disorderly

sà-rùp สรุป to summarize, sum up

sà-thǎa-nii-rót-fai สถานีรถไฟ train station

sà-thǎa-nii-tam-rùat สถานีตำรวจ police station

sà-thǎan-thôut สถาน ทูต embassy

sàt-trou ศัตรู enemy

sà-wàang สว่าง bright, brilliant (light)

sà-wâay-náam สระว่าย น้ำ swimming pool

sà-wàt-dii สวัสดี hello

sâwm ซ่อม to repair

sâwm ส้อม fork

sâwn ซ่อน to hide, conceal

sǎwn สอน to teach

sǎwng สอง two

sǐa เสีย to be broken, out of order, spoiled; to have gone off (food); to spend, pay; to be dead, (v) to die

sǐa-daay เสียดาย to regret, be sorry; "what a shame," "too bad"

sǐa-jai เสียใจ to be sad

sìang เสี่ยง to risk, take a risk, take a chance

sǐa-sà-là เสียสละ to sacrifice, give up (something)

sǐa-we-laa เสียเวลา to waste time

sǐi สี color

sìi สี่ four

sǐng-hǎa-khom สิงหาคม August

sòk-kà-pròk สกปรก dirty, filthy

sôm ส้ม orange

sòng ส่ง to send

sŏng-săi สงสัย to doubt, suspect

sŏn-jai สนใจ to be interested

sòt โสด single, unmarried

sôu สู้ to fight (physically), fight back, oppose, resist

sŏun ศูนย์ zero, center

sŏung สูง to be tall

sûam ส้วม toilet

sŭan สวน garden, park

sŭay สวย to be beautiful

súe ซื้อ to buy

sŭea เสือ tiger

sûea เสื้อ shirt

su-phâap สุภาพ to be polite, courteous

T

taa ตา eyes, maternal grandfather

tàang-châat ต่างชาติ alien, foreign (e.g. people)

tàang-prà-thêt ต่างประเทศ abroad

taay ตาย to die, pass away

tàe แต่ but

taeng-mo แตงโม watermelon

tàeng-ngaan แต่งงาน to marry, get married

tàeng-tua แต่งตัว to get dressed

tâi ใต้ under, south

tà-kìap ตะเกียบ chopstick(s)

tà-kon ตะโกน to cry out, shout, yell

tà-làat ตลาด market

tà-làwt ตลอด always, all the time

tà-lòk ตลก funny, comical, ridiculous

tam-bon ตำบล subdistrict: an administrative unit in Thailand

tam-rùat ตำรวจ policeman

tâng-jai ตั้งใจ to intend, pay attention

tâo-hôu เต้าหู้ beancurd, tofu

tao-òp เตาอบ oven

tao-rîit เตารีด iron

tàt ตัด to cut, cut off

tàt-phŏm ตัดผม to have a haircut

tàt-sĭn-jai ตัดสินใจ to decide, make decision

tawn-bàay ตอนบ่าย in the afternoon

tawn-cháo ตอนเช้า in the morning

tawn-kâm ตอนค่ำ at night

tawn-yen ตอนเย็น in the evening

tên เต้น to dance

tii ตี to hit, to beat; an hour of the morning from 1–5 a.m.

tìt ติด to stick, to get stuck; to be addicted to; to be close to; to owe, be owed

tìt-tàw ติดต่อ to communicate with, contact; contagious, infectious

tó โต๊ะ table, desk

toem เติม to add, put in (e.g. petrol)

tòk ตก to fall, to drop, diminish, decrease

tòk-jai ตกใจ alarmed, startled

tòk-long ตกลง to agree

tôm ต้ม to boil

tôu ตู้ cabinet

tôu-năng-sŭe ตู้หนังสือ bookshelf

tôu-sûea-phâa ตู้เสื้อผ้า closet

triam เตรียม prepare

trong-khâam ตรงข้าม across from

trong-pai ตรงไป go straight

trong-we-laa ตรงเวลา (to be) on time, punctual

trùat ตรวจ to inspect, examine, check

tua ตัว classifier for animals and objects

tŭa ตั๋ว ticket (for transport, entertainment)

tuean เตือน to remind, warn

tùen-nawn ตื่นนอน to get up

tùen-tên ตื่นเต้น to be excited; exciting

tù-laa-khom ตุลาคม October

tûm-hŏu ตุ้มหู earring(s)

Th

thâa ถ้า if

thăam ถาม to ask, enquire

thaan ทาน (formal) to eat (also drink)

thaang ทาง way, path, direction

thaang-àwk ทางออก exit, way out

thaang-khâo ทางเข้า entrance, way in

thăa-wawn ถาวร permanent, fixed, enduring

thàay-rôup ถ่ายรูป to photograph

thâeng แท่ง classifier for small tube-shaped items

thai ไทย Thai

thák-thaay ทักทาย to greet; to say hello

thá-láw ทะเลาะ to argue, an argument

thá-le ทะเล beach, sea

tham ทำ to do, make

tham-aa-hăan ทำอาหาร to cook

tham-khwaam-sà-àat ทำความสะอาด to clean

tham-laay ทำลาย to destroy, demolish, ruin

tham-má-châat ธรรมชาติ nature, natural

tham-má-daa ธรรมดา ordinary, common, simple, normal, undistinguished

tham-mai ทำไม why

tham-naay ทำนาย to predict, foretell, prophesy

tham-ngaan ทำงาน to work

tham-phìt ทำผิด (to do something morally) wrong

tham-ráay ทำร้าย to harm, injure, hurt

than ทัน in time (e.g. to get the bus)

thá-naa-kaan ธนาคาร bank

tháng-mòt ทั้งหมด altogether, all, the whole lot

than-sà-măi ทันสมัย to be modern, contemporary

than-waa-khom ธันวาคม December

tháo เท้า foot

tháo-kan เท่ากัน equal (e.g. amounts of something)

thâo-thiam เท่าเทียม to be equal

that-sà-ná-khá-tì ทัศนคติ opinion, view, attitude

thăwn ถอน to withdraw (e.g. money from the bank), to pull out, (e.g. a tooth)

thawng ทอง gold

tháwng ท้อง stomach; to be pregnant

tháwng-sĭa ท้องเสีย diarrhea

thàwt ถอด to take off, remove (clothes, shoes)

thĭang เถียง to argue, dispute, bicker

thîang-khuen เที่ยงคืน midnight

thîang-wan เที่ยงวัน noon

thîao bin เที่ยวบิน a flight (on a plane)

thîi ที่ at, place

thîi-năi ที่ไหน Where?

thîi-nân ที่นั่น there

thîi-nâng ที่นั่ง a seat, a place to sit

thîi-nawn ที่นอน a mattress

thîi-nîi ที่นี่ here

thîi-sùt ที่สุด the most, extremely

thîi-tham-ngaan ที่ทำงาน place of work, office, etc

thii-wii ทีวี television

thîi-yòu ที่อยู่ address

thíng ทิ้ง to throw away; desert, abandon

thon ทน to put up with, tolerate, bear

tho-rá-sàp โทรศัพท์ phone

thǒu ถู to rub, scrub, polish, wipe, clean (e.g. the floor)

thòuk ถูก to be cheap, inexpensive; to be right, correct; to touch

thǔe ถือ to hold something (in the hands)

thǔeng ถึง to reach, arrive (at), get to

thúk-khon ทุกคน everybody, everyone

thúk-khuen ทุกคืน every night, nightly

thúk-thîi ทุกที่ everywhere

thúk-wan ทุกวัน every day

thúk-yàang ทุกอย่าง everything

thûm ทุ่ม an hour of the night from 7-11 p.m.

thûng-tháo ถุงเท้า socks

thú-rá ธุระ business, work, something to do

U

ûan อ้วน to be fat

ùat อวด to show off, strut, flaunt

ù-bàt-tì-hèt อุบัติเหตุ accident

ûm อุ้ม to carry (e.g. a baby), hold in one's arms

ùn อุ่น to heat, warm

un-hà-phoum อุณหภูมิ temperature

ùp-pà-sàk อุปสรรค obstacle, difficulty, impediment

ùt-jaa-rá อุจจาระ (formal medical term) feces, stool, excrement

W

wâa ว่า that (used in reported speech)

waang วาง to lay (something) down, to put (something) down

wâang ว่าง to be unoccupied, vacant, free

wâang-ngaan ว่างงาน to be unemployed, jobless

wâat-rôup วาดรูป to draw/paint a picture

wâay-nám ว่ายน้ำ to swim

wâen แว่น glasses

wǎen แหวน a ring (jewelry)

wan วัน day

wǎng หวัง to hope

wan-kàwn วันก่อน the other day

wan-níi วันนี้ today

wan-yùt วันหยุด day off

wàt หวัด common cold

wát วัด temple

we-laa เวลา time, at the time

we-laa-wâang เวลาว่าง free time

wí-chaa วิชา subject of study

wí-naa-thii วินาที second

wîng วิ่ง to run

wít-thá-yú วิทยุ radio

wiw วิว view

wong-don-trii วงดนตรี (a musical) band

woy-waay โวยวาย to make a fuss, to complain (animatedly)

wua วัว cow, cattle

wún วุ้น jelly, gelatin

wún-sên วุ้นเส้น clear noodles

wûn-waay วุ่นวาย to be busy (crowded), chaotic, turbulent

Y

yaa ยา medicine, drug

yàa อย่า don't (do that)!

yàa หย่า to divorce

yâa ย่า paternal grandmother

yàak อยาก to want, desire, need, require

yâak ยาก to be difficult

yaam ยาม security guard

yàap-khaay หยาบคาย to be rude, crude

yaa-sà-phŏm ยาสระ ผม shampoo

yaa-sĭi-fan ยาสีฟัน toothpaste

yaaw ยาว to be long

yaay ยาย maternal grandmother

yáay ย้าย to move (from one place to another), transfer, shift

yâe แย่ to be terrible

yâek แยก to separate, divide, split, spread apart

yâeng แย่ง to grab, snatch; scramble for; vie/compete (for)

yài ใหญ่ to be big

yam ยำ Thai-style spicy salad

yang-ngai ยังไง How?, In what way?

yáp ยับ wrinkled (clothing), crushed

yawm ยอม to yield, give in, submit; to allow, consent

yawm-pháe ยอมแพ้ to surrender, give up, give in (to)

yawm-ráp ยอมรับ to acknowledge, accept, agree; to admit, confess

yâwt-yîam ยอดเยี่ยม to be excellent

yen เย็น to be cool; evening

yîam เยี่ยม to visit, call on, go to see (someone)

yím ยิ้ม to smile

ying ยิง to shoot

yìng หยิ่ง (to be) haughty, conceited, vain, proud, aloof

yĭng หญิง woman, female

yóe เยอะ to be a lot, plenty

yók-lôek ยกเลิก cancel (e.g. a contract)

yók-thôt ยกโทษ to forgive, pardon

yók-wén ยกเว้น to except, excluding, not including; exempt

yòu อยู่ to live, stay

yú ยุ to incite, provoke

yuem ยืม to borrow

yuen ยืน to stand, get on one's feet

yung ยุง mosquito

yûng ยุ่ง to be busy/ hectic (work, etc.); to interfere meddle

yùt หยุด to stop, halt

yút-tì-tham ยุติธรรม to be just, fair

English–Thai Glossary

A

about *kìaw-kàp*
เกี่ยวกับ

above *nǔea* เหนือ

accident *ù-bàt-tì-hèt*
อุบัติเหตุ

accommodation
thîi-phák ที่พัก

ache, be in pain *pùat*
ปวด

across *trong-khâam*
ตรงข้าม

add *sài, phôem* ใส่,
เพิ่ม

address *thîi-yòu* ที่อยู่

adorable *nâa-rák*
น่ารัก

advise *náe-nam* แนะนำ

afraid, scared *klua* กลัว

Africa *áp-frí-kaa*
แอฟริกา

afternoon *tawn-bàay*
ตอนบ่าย

again *ìik* อีก

age *aa-yú* อายุ

agree (with someone)
hěn-dûay เห็นด้วย

ago *thîi-láew* ที่แล้ว

air *aa-kàat* อากาศ

airplane *khrûeang-bin*
เครื่องบิน

airport *sà-nǎam-bin*
สนามบิน

alcohol *lâo* เหล้า

all *tháng-mòt* ทั้งหมด

allergic; allergy *pháe*
แพ้

almost *kùeap* เกือบ

alone (be by oneself)
khon-diaw คนเดียว

already *láew* แล้ว

also, too *dûay* ด้วย

ambulance *rót-phá-yaa-baan* รถพยาบาล

America *à-me-rí-kaa*
อเมริกา

amusing, funny *tà-lòk*
ตลก

and *láe, kàp* และ, กับ

angry *kròt* โกรธ

animal *sàt* สัตว์

annoy *ram-khaan*
รำคาญ

another *ùean, ìik* อื่น,
อีก

apartment *hǎw-phák*
หอพัก

apologize *khǎw -thôt*
ขอโทษ

appearance *nâa-taa*
หน้าตา

apply (for a job) *sà-màk*
สมัคร

appointment *nát-mǎay*
นัดหมาย

appreciate; thank you
khàwp-khun ขอบคุณ

appropriate, suitable
màw-sǒm เหมาะสม

April *me-sǎa-yon*
เมษายน

are *pen, yòu* เป็น, อยู่

arm *khǎen* แขน

arrange *jàt-kaan*
จัดการ

arrive *maa-thǔeng*
มาถึง

ask (a question) *thǎam*
ถาม

ask for, request *khǎw*
ขอ

assist *châuy* ช่วย

at *thîi* ที่

ATM *tôu-e-thii-em*
ตู้เอทีเอ็ม

August *sǐng-hǎa-khom*
สิงหาคม

Australia *áws-tre-lia*
ออสเตรเลีย

available, free (not busy)
wâang ว่าง

B

back (part of body) *lăng*
หลัง

bad *lew* เลว

bag (paper or plastic)
thŭng ถุง

baht (Thai currency)
bàat บาท

bake *òp* อบ

banana *klûay* กล้วย

band (of musicians)
wong-don-trii วง
ดนตรี

Bangkok *krung-thêp*
กรุงเทพฯ

bank *thá-naa-kaan*
ธนาคาร

bank account book
sà-mùt-ban-chii สมุด
บัญช

barber *châang-tàt-
phŏm* ช่างตัดผม

bath *àap-nám* อาบน้ำ

bathroom *hâwng-náam*
ห้องน้ำ

bathtub *àang-àap-náam*
อ่างอาบน้ำ

beach, sea *thá-le* ทะเล

beat (strike) *tii* ตี

beautiful *sŭay* สวย

because *phráw* เพราะ

bed *tiang* เตียง

bedroom *hâwng-nawn*
ห้องนอน

bed sheet *phâa-pou-thîi-
nawn* ผ้าปูที่นอน

beef *nûea-wua* เนื้อวัว

before *kàwn* ก่อน

begin *rôem* เริ่ม

behind *khâang-lăng*
ข้างหลัง

believe *chûea* เชื่อ

best *dii-thîi-sùt* ดีที่สุด

better *dii-kwàa* ดีกว่า

between *rá-wàang*
ระหว่าง

bicycle *jàk-krà-yaan*
จักรยาน

big *yài* ใหญ่

bird *nók* นก

birthday *wan-kòet*
วันเกิด

bit *nít-nòi* นิดหน่อย

black *sĭi-dam* สีดำ

blanket *phâa-hòm*
ผ้าห่ม

blood *lûeat* เลือด

blue (dark) *sĭi-náam-
ngoen* สีน้ำเงิน

blue (light) *sĭi-fáa* สีฟ้า

boat,ship *ruea* เรือ

body *râang-kaay, tua*
รางกาย, ตัว

boil *tôm* ต้ม

book *năng-sŭe* หนังสือ

bookstore *ráan-năng-
sŭe* ร้านหนังสือ

born *kòet* เกิด

borrow *yuem* ยืม

bottle *khùat* ขวด

bowl *chaam* ชาม

boyfriend/girlfriend
faen แฟน

bread *khà-nŏm-pang*
ขนมปัง

breakfast *aa-hăan-cháo*
อาหารเช้า

bride *jâo-săaw* เจ้าสาว

bridegroom *jâo-bàaw*
เจ้าบาว

bridge *sà-phaan*
สะพาน

bring up/raise (children)
líang เลี้ยง

British *kon-ang-krìt*
คนอังกฤษ

broken *sĭa* เสีย

brother (older) *phîi-
chaay* พี่ชาย

brother (younger)
náwng-chaay น้องชาย

brown *sĭi-náam-taan*
สีน้ำตาล

brush teeth *praeng-fan*
แปรงฟัน

buddy *phûean* เพื่อน

building (noun) *tùek*
ตึก

burn *phăo* เผา

but *tàe* แต่

butter *noei* เนย

buy *súe* ซื้อ

C

cabbage *kà-làm-plii* กะหล่ำปลี

cabinet *tôu* ตู้

calculator *khrûeang-khít-lêk* เครื่องคิดเลข

call, summon *rîak* เรียก

Canada *khae-naa-daa* แคนาดา

cancel *yók-lôek* ยกเลิก

cancer *má-reng* มะเร็ง

candle *thian* เทียน

cap, hat *mùak* หมวก

car *rót* รถ

careful *rá-wang* ระวัง

carry (in the hands) *hîw* หิ้ว, ถือ

cash (money) *ngoen-sòt* เงินสด

cat *maew* แมว

catch *jàp* จับ

cattle *wua* วัว

celebrate *chà-lǎwng* ฉลอง

cell phone *mue-thǔe* มือถือ

certain *nae-nawn* แนนอน

chair *kôa-îi* เก้าอี้

chance, opportunity *o-kàat* โอกาส

change (clothes, plans) *plian* เปลี่ยน

change one's mind *plian-jai* เปลี่ยนใจ

chat *khuy* คุย

cheap (price) *thòuk* ถูก

cheat *kong* โกง

check, verify *chék, trùat-sàwp* เช็ค, ตรวจสอบ

chicken *kài* ไก่

child (son or daughter) *lôuk* ลูก

chili pepper *prík* พริก

chilly (weather) *nǎaw* หนาว

China *jiin* จีน

Chinese *phaa-sǎa-jiin* ภาษาจีน

cigarette *bù-rii* บุหรี่

city, large town *mueang* เมือง

class *rian* เรียน

clean *sà-àat* สะอาด

clean (verb) *tham-khwaam-sà-àat* ทำความสะอาด

clever *chà-làat* ฉลาด

client, customer *lôuk-kháa* ลูกค้า

clothes, clothing *sûea-phâa* เสื้อผ้า

coconut *má-práow* มะพร้าว

coconut milk *krà-thí* กระทิ

code *rá-hàt* รหัส

cold (drink) *yen* เย็น

cold (weather) *nǎaw* หนาว

color *sǐi* สี

comb *wǐi* หวี

come *maa* มา

come back *klàp-maa* กลับมา

come from *maa-jàak* มาจาก

comfortable *sà-baay* สบาย

company *baw-rí-sàt* บริษัท

compete, to *khàeng* แข่ง

complain, to *bòn* บ่น

computer *khawm-phíew-tôe* คอมพิวเตอร์

confident *mân-jai* มั่นใจ

confused *ngong* งง

connect *tàw* ต่อ

consult, talk over with *prùek-sǎa* ปรึกษา

control (verb) *khûap-khum* ควบคุม

convenient *sà-dùak* สะดวก

cook *tham-aa-hǎan* ทำอาหาร

cool *yen* เย็น

corn *khâo-phôt* ข้าวโพด

corner *mum* มุม

correct; to be right *thòuk-tâwng* ถูกต้อง

correct (an error) *kâe* แก้

cost (price) *raa-khaa* ราคา

country *prà-thêt* ประเทศ

court (of law) *săan* ศาล

cow *wua* วัว

crab *pou* ปู

cramp (muscle pain) *tà-kriw* ตะคริว

crash *chon* ชน

crazy, mad *bâa* บ้า

create, build *sâang* สร้าง

credit card *bàt-khre-dìt* บัตรเครดิต

cry (shed tears) *ráwng-hâi* ร้องไห้

cucumber *taeng-kwaa* แตงกวา

cup *thûay* ถ้วย

cure/treat (an illness) *rák-săa* รักษา

curious *sŏng-sai* สงสัย

cushion, pillow *măwn* หมอน

cut *tàt* ตัด

cut (injure) *phlăe* แผล

cute *nâa-rák* น่ารัก

D

dam *khùean* เขื่อน

dance *tên* เต้น

danger, dangerous *an-tà-raay* อันตราย

dark (color) *khêm* เข้ม

dark (complexion) *khlâm* คล้ำ

dark (night) *mûet* มืด

daughter *lôuk-săaw* ลูกสาว

day *wan* วัน

day off *wan-yùt* วันหยุด

dead *taay* ตาย

debt *nîi* หนี้

December *than-waa-khom* ธันวาคม

decorate *tàeng* แต่ง

deep *lúek* ลึก

delay *cháa* ช้า

delete *lóp* ลบ

delicious *à-ròi* อร่อย

deliver *sòng* ส่ง

dentist *than-tà-phâet* ทันตแพทย์

depart *àwk-jàak* ออกจาก

department store *hâang* ห้าง

deposit money *fàak-ngoen* ฝากเงิน

desk *tóe* โต๊ะ

dessert *khà-nŏm* ขนม

develop *phát-thá-naa* พัฒนา

die *taay* ตาย

difficult *yàak* ยาก

dinner *aa-hăan-yen* อาหารเย็น

dirt *din* ดิน

dirty *sòk-kà-pròk* สกปรก

disappointed *phìt-wăng* ผิดหวัง

discount *lót* ลด

disease *rôk* โรค

dish, plate *jaan* จาน

dislike *mâi-châwp* ไม่ชอบ

dive *dam-náam* ดำน้ำ

divorce *yàa* หย่า

do *tham* ทำ

doctor *măw* หมอ

dog *măa* หมา

dollar *dawn-lâa* ดอลลาร์

don't! (do something) *yàa* อย่า

door *prà-tou* ประตู

down *long* ลง

downstairs *khâang-lâang* ข้างล่าง

drama (soap opera) *lá-khawn* ละคร

draw (a picture) *wâat* วาด

dream *făn* ฝัน

drink *dùem* ดื่ม

drive *khàp* ขับ

driver *khon-khàp-rót*
คนขับ

dry *hâeng* แห้ง

duck *pèt* เป็ด

E

ears *hǒu* หู

earth, soil *din* ดิน

easy *ngâay* ง่าย

eat *kin* กิน

eggs *khài* ไข่

eight *pàet* แปด

elbow *khâw-sàwk*
ข้อศอก

electric, electricity
fai-fáa ไฟฟ้า

elephant *cháang* ช้าง

eleven *sìp-èt* สิบเอ็ด

email *ii-meo* อีเมล์

embarrassing *nâa-aay*
นาอาย

embassy *sà-thǎan-thôut*
สถานทูต

embrace, hug *ka-wt*
กอด

emergency *chùk-chǒen*
ฉุกเฉิน

empty *wàang* ว่าง

end (ending) *jòp* จบ

engaged (to be married)
mân หมั้น

English *phaaa-sǎa-ang-
krìt* ภาษาอังกฤษ

England *ang-krìt*
อังกฤษ

enjoy, fun *sànùk* สนุก

enough, sufficient
phaw พอ

enter *khâo* เข้า

entrance *thaang-khâo*
ทางเข้า

envelope *song* ซอง

equal *thâo* เท่า

errand *thù-rá* ธุระ

evening *tawn-yen*
ตอนเย็น

every *thúk* ทุก

every day *thúk-wan*
ทุกวัน

everyone *thúk-khon*
ทุกคน

everything *thúk-yàang*
ทุกอย่าง

exam, test *sàwp* สอบ

exchange (money)
lâek-ngoen แลกเงิน

excited *tùen-tên*
ตื่นเต้น

exercise (verb) *àwk-
kam-lang kaay*
ออกกำลังกาย

exit *thaang-àwk*
ทางออก

expense(s) *ray-jàay*
รายจ่าย

expensive *phaeng* แพง

experience *prà-sòp-
kaan* ประสบการณ์

extra *phí-sèt* พิเศษ

extremely *thîi-sùt*
ที่สุด

eye *taa* ตา

F

face *nǎa* หน้า

faint *pen-lom* เป็นลม

fake (imitation) *plawm*
ปลอม

fall *tòk* ตก

fall over *lóm* ล้ม

family *khrâwp-khrua*
ครอบครัว

fan *phát-lom* พัดลม

fancy *rǔu* หรู

far *klai* ไกล

farmer *chaaw-naa*
ชาวนา

fast *reo* เร็ว

fat *ûan* อ้วน

father *phâw* พ่อ

fear *klua* กลัว

fee *khâa* ค่า

feel *róu-sùek* รู้สึก

fever *pen-khâi* เป็นไข้

fiancé(e) *khôu-mân*
คู่หมั้น

field, lawn *sà-nǎam*
สนาม

field, paddy *naa* นา

fight *sôu* สู้

finger *níw* นิ้ว

finished *sèt* เสร็จ

fire *fai* ไฟ

fish *plaa* ปลา

fish sauce *nám-plaa*
น้ำปลา

five *hâa* ห้า

fix, repair *sâwm* ซ่อม

flashlight, torch *fai-chăay* ไฟฉาย

flesh, meat *núea* เนื้อ

flight (airline) *thîaw-bin* เที่ยวบิน

flirt *jìip* จีบ

float *loy* ลอย

flood *nám-thûam* น้ำท่วม

floor *phúen* พื้น

flour *pâeng* แป้ง

flower *dàwk-mái* ดอกไม้

flu *khâi-wàt-yài* ไข้หวัดใหญ่

fly (insect) *má-laeng-wan* แมลงวัน

fly (verb) *bin* บิน

fond of *châwp* ชอบ

food *aa-hăan* อาหาร

foot *tháo* เท้า

foreign *tàang-prà-thêt* ต่างประเทศ

forest *pàa* ป่า

forget *luem* ลืม

fork *sâwm* ส้อม

four *sìi* สี่

France *fà-ràng-sèt* ฝรั่งเศส

French *phaa-săa-fà-ràng-sèt* ภาษาฝรั่งเศส

fresh *sòt* สด

Friday *wan-sùk* วันศุกร์

friend *phûean* เพื่อน

frightened *tòk-jai* ตกใจ

from *jàak* จาก

front *nâa* หน้า

fruit *phŏn-lá-mái* ผลไม้

fry *thâwt* ทอด

full *ìm* อิ่ม

fun *sà-nùk* สนุก

funny *tà-lòk* ตลก

future *à-naa-khót* อนาคต

G

garage (for parking) *rong-rót* โรงรถ

garbage *khà-yà* ขยะ

garden, yard *sŭan* สวน

garlic *krà-thiam* กระเทียม

gas, gasoline, petrol *nám-man* น้ำมัน

gas station *pám-nám-man* ปั๊มน้ำมัน

generous *jai-dee* ใจดี

German *phaa-săa-yoe-rá-man* ภาษาเยอรมัน

Germany *yoe-rá-man* เยอรมัน

get (receive) *dâi* ได้

get off (e.g. a bus) *long* ลง

get on (e.g. a bus) *khûen* ขึ้น

get up *tùen-nawn* ตื่นนอน

get well *hăay* หาย

gift, present *khăwng-khwăn* ของขวัญ

ginger *khĭng* ขิง

girl (child) *dèk-phôu-yĭng* เด็กผู้หญิง

girlfriend/boyfriend *faehn* แฟน

give *hâi* ให้

glad *dii-jai* ดีใจ

glass *kâew* แก้ว

glasses *wâen-taa* แว่นตา

glue *kaaw* กาว

go *pai* ไป

go back *klàp* กลับ

go home *klàp-bâan* กลับบ้าน

go out *pai-thîaw* ไปเที่ยว

go straight ahead *trong-pai* ตรงไป

go to work *pai-tham-ngaan* ไปทำงาน

gold (precious metal) *thawng* ทอง

gold (color) *sĭi-thawng* สีทอง

good *dii* ดี

government *rát-thà-baan* รัฐบาล

grandchild *lǎan* หลาน

granddaughter *lǎan-sǎaw* หลานสาว

grandfather (maternal) *taa* ตา

grandfather (paternal) *pòu* ปู่

grandmother (maternal) *yaay* ยาย

grandmother (paternal) *yâa* ย่า

grandson *lǎan-chaay* หลานชาย

grape *à-ngùn* องุ่น

grass *yâa* หญ้า

grateful *khàwp-khun* ขอบคุณ

gray *sǐi-thao* สีเทา

green *sǐi-khǐaw* สีเขียว

green bean *thùa-fàk-yaaw* ถั่วฝักยาว

grill *yàang* ย่าง

group กลุ่ม

guava *fà-ràng* ฝรั่ง

guest *khàek* แขก

H

hair *phǒm* ผม

haircut *tàt-phǒm* ตัดผม

half *khrûeng* ครึ่ง

hand *mue* มือ

handsome *làw* หล่อ

hang up (the phone) *waang-sǎay* วางสาย

happy *dii-jai* ดีใจ

hard (difficult) *yâak* ยาก

hard (solid) *khǎeng* แข็ง

hardworking *khà-yǎn* ขยัน

hat, cap *mùak* หมวก

hate *klìat* เกลียด

have, has *mii* มี

he *khǎo* เขา

head *hǔa* หัว

heal *rák-sǎa* รักษา

health *sùk-khà-phâap* สุขภาพ

hear *dâi-yin* ได้ยิน

heart *hǔa-jai* หัวใจ

heart attack *hǔa-jai-waay* หัวใจวาย

heavy *nàk* หนัก

hello *sà-wàt-dii* สวัสดี

hello (on phone) *han-lǒ* ฮัลโหล

help *chûay* ช่วย

her *khǎo* เขา

here *thîi-nîi* ที่นี่

here it is *nîi khâ/khráp* นี่ ค่ะ/ครับ

him *khǎo* เขา

his *khǎwng-khǎo* ของเขา

hit *tii* ตี

hold the line *raw-sàk-krôu* รอสักครู่

home *bâan* บ้าน

homework *kaan-bâan* การบ้าน

honey *náam-phûeng* น้ำผึ้ง

hope *wǎng* หวัง

hospital *rong-phá-yaa-baan* โรงพยาบาล

hot *ráwn* ร้อน

hotel *rong-raem* โรงแรม

hour *chûa-mong* ชั่วโมง

house *bâan* บ้าน

housekeeper, housemaid *mâe-bâan* แม่บ้าน

how *yang-ngai* ยังไง

How many? *kìi* กี่

How much? *thâo-rài* เท่าไร

How old? *kìi-pii* กี่ปี

huge *yài* ใหญ่

humid *chúen* ชื้น

humorous, funny *tà-lòk* ตลก

hundred *rói* ร้อย

hungry *hǐw* หิว

Hurry up! *reo-reo* เร็วๆ

husband *sǎa-mii* สามี

hurt (injured), sore *jèp* เจ็บ

I

I (female) *chăn* ฉัน

I (male) *phŏm* ผม

ice *nám-khăeng* น้ำแข็ง

ice cream *ai-sà-khriim* ไอศกรีม

iced water *nám-yen* น้ำเย็น

if *thâa* ถ้า

ill, sick *mâi-sà-baay* ไม่สบาย

image *rôup-phâap* รูปภาพ

immediately *than-thii* ทันที

impatient *jai-ráwn* ใจร้อน

important *săm-khan* สำคัญ

impressive *prà-tháp-jai* ประทับใจ

in *nai* ใน

in front *khâang-nâa* ข้างหน้า

in order to *phûea* เพื่อ

incense stick *thôup* ธูป

inconvenient *mâi-sà-dùak* ไม่สะดวก

incredible (exclamation) *mâi-nâa-chûea* ไม่น่าเชื่อ

India *in-dia* อินเดีย

Indian *khon-in-dia* คนอินเดีย

inexpensive *mâi-phaeng* ไม่แพง

inform *jâeng* แจ้ง

information, data *khâw-moun* ข้อมูล

ingredient *khrûeang-prung* เครื่องปรุง

injection *chìit-yaa* ฉีดยา

injured *bàat-jèp* บาดเจ็บ

insect *má-laeng* แมลง

inside *khâang-nai* ข้างใน

insult *dou-thòuk* ดูถูก

intend *tang-jai* ตั้งใจ

interested (in) *sŏn-jai* สนใจ

Internet *in-toe-nèt* อินเตอร์เน็ต

interpret, translate *plae* แปล

interpreter *lâam* ล่าม

intersection *sìi-yâek* สี่แยก

interview *săm-phâat* สัมภาษณ์

introduce *náe-nam* แนะนำ

invite (informal) *chuan* ชวน

invite (formal) *choen* เชิญ

is *pen, yòu* เป็น, อยู่

island *kàw* เกาะ

Italy *i-taa-lii* อิตาลี

Italian *phaa-săa-i-taa-lii* ภาษาอิตาลี

itchy *khan* คัน

J

jam *yaem* แยม

January *mók-kà-raa-khom* มกราคม

Japan *yîi-pùn* ญี่ปุ่น

Japanese *phaa-săa-yîi-pùn* ภาษาญี่ปุ่น

jeans *kaang-keng-yiin* กางเกงยีน

joke (with someone) *phôut-lên* พูดเลน

journalist *nák-khàaw* นักข่าว

juice *nám-phŏn-lá-mái* น้ำผลไม้

July *kà-rá-kà-daa-khom* กรกฎาคม

jump *krà-dòt* กระโดด

June *mí-thù-naa-yon* มิถุนายน

jungle *pàa* ป่า

just now *phôeng* เพิ่ง

K

kale *khá-náa* คะน้า

keep *kèp* เก็บ

kettle *kaa-nám* กาน้ำ

key (for a room) *kun-jae* กุญแจ

kick *tè* เตะ

kid (child) *dèk* เด็ก

kidney *tai* ไต

kill *khâa* ฆ่า

kilogram *kì-lo-kram* กิโลกรัม

kind (personality) *jai-dii* ใจดี

kindergarten *rong-rian-à-nú-baan* โรงเรียนอนุบาล

kiss (verb) *jòup* จูบ

kitchen *khrua* ครัว

knee *khào* เข่า

knife *mîit* มีด

know (something) *rúu* รู้

know (someone) *rúu-jàk* รู้จัก

Korea *kao-lǐi* เกาหลี

Korean *phaa-sǎa-kao-lǐi* ภาษาเกาหลี

L

lamp *khom* โคมไฟ

land, property *thîi-din* ที่ดิน

language *phaa-sǎa* ภาษา

large, big *yài* ใหญ่

last *thîi-lâew* ที่แล้ว

late *sǎay* สาย

late at night *dùek* ดึก

laugh *hǔa-ró* หัวเราะ

laundry *sák-phâa* ซักผ้า

lawyer *thá-naay-khwaam* ทนายความ

leak *rûa* รั่ว

learn, study *rian* เรียน

leather *nǎng* หนัง

leave a message *fàk-khâw-khwaam* ฝากข้อความ

leg *khǎa* ขา

lemongrass *tà-khrái* ตะไคร้

lend *hâi-yuem* ให้ยืม

letter (mail) *jòt-mǎay* จดหมาย

lettuce *phàk-kàat-khǎaw* ผักกาดขาว

library *hâwng-sà-mùt* ห้องสมุด

lid (of a jar) *fǎa* ฝา

lie down *nawn* นอน

life *chii-wít* ชีวิต

lift, raise *yók* ยก

light (color) *àwn* อ่อน

light (bright) *sà-wàang* สว่าง

light (lamp) *fai* ไฟ

like *châwp* ชอบ

lime *má-naaw* มะนาว

lip *rim-fǐi-pàak* ริมฝีปาก

liquor, alcohol *lâo* เหล้า

listen *fang* ฟัง

little *nít-nòi, nói* นิด หน่อย, น้อย

live *yùu* อยู่

living room *hông-nâng-lên* ห้องนั่งเล่น

long *yaaw* ยาว

look at *dou* ดู

look for, search, look up *hǎa* หา

lose, be defeated *phâe* แพ้

lost *hǎay* หาย

lot (a large amount) *mâak, yóe* มาก, เยอะ

loud *dang* ดัง

love (verb) *rák* รัก

lovely, adorable *nâa-ák* น่ารัก

lucky *chôk-dii* โชคดี

luggage, bag, suitcase *krà-pǎo* กระเป๋า

lunch *aa-hǎan-thîang* อาหารเที่ยง

M

make *tham* ทำ

makeup (cosmetics) *khrûeang-sǎm-aang* เครื่องสำอาง

man/men *phôu-chaay* ผู้ชาย

manager *phôu-jàt-kaan* ผู้จัดการ

mango *má-mûang* มะม่วง

mangosteen (fruit) *mang-khút* มังคุด

manners *maa-rá-yâat* มารยาท

many *mâak* มาก

map *phǎen-thîi* แผนที่

March *mii-naa-khom* มีนาคม

market *tà-làat* ตลาด

marry, get married *tàeng-ngaan* แต่งงาน

massage *nûat* นวด

mattress *thîi-nawn* ที่นอน

May *phrúet-sà-phaa-khom* พฤษภาคม

me (female) *chǎn* ฉัน

me (male) *phǒm* ผม

measure *wát* วัด

meat, flesh *núea* นื้อ

medicine, drug *yaa* ยา

meet *phóp* พบ

meeting, conference *prà-chum* ประชุม

message *khâw-khwaam* ข้อความ

method *wí-thii* วิธี

midday *thîang-wan* เที่ยงวัน

midnight *thîang-khuen* เที่ยงคืน

milk (also used for a woman's breasts) *nom* นม

million *láan* ล้าน

mincemeat *sàp* สับ

mind *jai* ใจ

mine (female) *khǎwng-chǎn* ของฉัน

mine (male) *khǎwng-phǒm* ของผม

minibus (with two bench seats) *rót-sǎwng-thǎew* รถสองแถว

ministry (government) *krà-suang* กระทรวง

minute *naa-thii* นาที

mirror, a *krà-jòk* กระจก

miss (someone) *khít-thǔeng* คิดถึง

mist, fog *màwk* หมอก

mix, blend (verb) *phà-sǒm* ผสม

mobile phone *mue-thǔe* มือถือ

Monday *wan-jan* วันจันทร์

money *ngoen* เงิน

monk (Buddhist) *phrá* พระ

monkey *ling* ลิง

month *duean* เดือน

morning *tawn-cháo* ตอนเช้า

mother, mom *mâe* แม่

mountain *phuu-khǎo* ภูเขา

moustache *nùat* หนวด

mouth *pàak* ปาก

movie *nǎng* หนัง

Mr./Mrs./Miss *Khun* คุณ

MSG (monosodium glutamate) *phǒng-chou-rót* ผงชูรส

museum *phí-phít-thá-phan* พิพิธภัณฑ์

mushroom(s) *hèt* เห็ด

music *phleng, dontrii* เพลงดนตรี

N

nail (finger, toe) *lép* เล็บ

name *chûe* ชื่อ

nation, country *prà-thêt* ประเทศ

navy blue *sǐi-nám-ngoen* สีน้ำเงิน

near *klâi* ใกล้

neck *khaw* คอ

neighbor *phûean-bâan* เพื่อนบ้าน

never mind *mâi-pen-rai* ไม่เป็นไร

new *mài* ใหม่

news *khàaw* ข่าว

newspaper *nǎang-sǔe-phim* หนังสือพิมพ์

New Zealand *niw-sii-laen* นิวซีแลนด์

nice, good *dii* ดี

nickname *chûe-lên* ชื่อเล่น

nighttime *tawn-khâm* ตอนค่ำ

nine *kâo* เก้า

nineteen *sìp-kâo* สิบ
เก้า

ninety *kâo-sìp* เก้าสิบ

no, not *mâi, mâi-châi*
ไม่, ไม่ใช่

noise, sound *sǐang*
เสียง

noisy, loud noise
sǐang-dang เสียงดัง

noodles *kǔay-tǐaw*
ก๋วยเตี๋ยว

noon *thîang-wan*
ตอนเที่ยง

normal *pòk-kà-tì* ปกติ

nose *jà-mòuk* จมูก

not at all *mâi-loei*
ไม่เลย

notebook *sà-mùt* สมุด

November *phrúet-sà-jì-
kaa-yon* พฤศจิกายน

now *tawn-níi* ตอนนี้

number *boe* เบอร์

nurse *phá-yaa-baan*
พยาบาล

O

o' clock *mong* โมง

October *tù-laa-khom*
ตุลาคม

of, belong to *khǎwng*
ของ

often *bòi* บ่อย

oil *nám-man* น้ำมัน

old *kào* เก่า

on *bon* บน

one *nùeng* หนึ่ง

one hundred *nùeng-rói*
หนึ่งร้อย

one hundred thousand
nùeng-sǎen หนึ่งแสน

one thousand *nùeng-
phan* หนึ่งพัน

one way *thîaw-diaw*
เที่ยวเดียว

onion *hǔa-hǎwm*
หัวหอม

open, turn on *pòet* เปิด

opposite *trong-khâam*
ตรงข้าม

or *rǔe* หรือ

orange *sôm* ส้ม

order *sàng* สั่ง

other *ùen* อื่น

our *khǎwng-rao* ของ
เรา

outside *khâang-nâwk*
ข้างนอก

oven *tao-òp* เตาอบ

overseas *tàang-prà-thêt*
ต่างประเทศ

ox *wua* วัว

P

page (in a book) *nâa*
หน้า

pain, painful *jèp* เจ็บ

pair *kôu* คู่

pajamas *chút-nawn*
ชุดนอน

pan, frying pan *krà-thá*
กระทะ

papaya *má-lá-kaw*
มะละกอ

papaya salad *sôm-tam*
ส้มตำ

paper *krà-dàat*
กระดาษ

parents *phâw-mâe*
พ่อแม่

park, public garden
sǔan สวน

passport *nǎng-sǔe-
doen-thaang*
หนังสือเดินทาง

patient (personality)
jai-yen ใจเย็น

pay *jàay* จ่าย

peanut *thùa* ถั่ว

pen *pàak-kaa* ปากกา

pencil *din-sǎw* ดินสอ

people, person *khon*
คน

pepper (chili pepper)
phrík พริก

perfume *nám-hǎwm*
น้ำหอม

pet (animal) *sàt-líang*
สัตว์เลี้ยง

petrol, gas *nám-man*
น้ำมัน

pick up (the phone)
ráp-sǎay รับสาย

picture, photo *rôup,
phâap* รูป, ภาพ

pig, pork *mŏu* หมู

pill(s) *yaa* ยา

pillow, cushion *măwn* หมอน

pineapple *sàp-pà-rót* สับปะรด

pink *sĭi-chom-phou* สีชมพู

plane *khrûeang-bin* เครื่องบิน

plant (verb) *plòuk* ปลูก

plate *jaan* จาน

play (verb) *lên* เล่น

playful *khîi-lên* ขี้เล่น

please *chûay* ช่วย

pleased *dii-jai* ดีใจ

plenty *mâak-maay* มากมาย

police *tam-rùat* ตำรวจ

police station *sà-thăa-nii-tam-rùat* สถานีตำรวจ

poor *jon* จน

port, harbor *thâa-ruea* ท่าเรือ

post office *prai-sà-nii* ไปรษณีย์

post, mail *jòt-măay* จดหมาย

pot, saucepan *mâw* หม้อ

prawn, shrimp *kûng* กุ้ง

prepare, make ready *triam* เตรียม

present, gift *khăwng-khwăn* ของขวัญ

pretty *sŭay* สวย

price *raa-khaa* ราคา

prize, reward *raang-wan* รางวัล

problem *pan-hăa* ปัญหา

professor *aa-jaan* อาจารย์

proficiently *kèng* เก่ง

promise *săn-yaa* สัญญา

proud *phoum-jai* ภูมิใจ

province *jang-wàt* จังหวัด

pull *dueng* ดึง

punctual, on time *trong-we-laa* ตรงเวลา

purple *sĭi-mûang* สีม่วง

purse *krá-păo* กระเป๋า

put on, wear *sài* ใส่

Q

question *kham-thăam* คำถาม

quickly *reo* เร็ว

quiet *ngîap* เงียบ

quit, give up *lôek* เลิก

quit, resign *laa-àwk* ลาออก

R

rabbit *krà-tàay* กระต่าย

radio *wít-thá-yú* วิทยุ

rain (noun) *fŏn* ฝน

rain (verb) *fŏn-tòk* ฝนตก

raise, breed *líang* เลี้ยง

rash *phùen* ผื่น

rat/mouse *nŏu* หนู

read *àan* อ่าน

ready *phrâwm* พร้อม

really, very *mâak* จมาก

receive *ráp* รับ

red *sĭi-daeng* สีแดง

reduce *lót* ลด

refrigerator *tôu-yen* ตู้เย็น

regret, feel sorry *sĭa-jai* เสียใจ

relatives *yâat* ญาติ

rent *châo* เช่า

reply *tàwp* ตอบ

request *khăw* ขอ

reserve (a room) *jawng* จอง

rest, relax *phák-phàwn* พักผ่อน

restaurant *ráan-aa-hăan* ร้านอาหาร

restroom (bathroom) *hâwng-nám* ห้องน้ำ

return, go back *klàp* กลับ

return a call *tho-klàp* โทรกลับ

rice (cooked) *khâaw* ข้าว

rice fields *naa* นา

rich, wealthy *ruay* รวย

ride (bicycle or animal) *khìi* ขี่

ring (jewelry) *wǎen* แหวน

rinse, wash *láang* ล้าง

river *mâe-náam* แม่น้ำ

road *thà-nǒn* ถนน

roast, grill *yâang* ย่าง

room (house/hotel) *hâwng* ห้อง

round trip *pai-klàp* ไปกลับ

run *wîng* วิ่ง

S

sad *sǐa-jai* เสียใจ

salary *ngoen-duean* เงินเดือน

sale (reduced prices) *lót-raa-khaa* ลดราคา

salt *kluea* เกลือ

salty *khem* เค็ม

same *mǔean* เหมือน

sandals *rawng-tháo-tàe* รองเท้าแตะ

Saturday *wan-sǎo* วันเสาร์

say, speak *phôut* พูด

school *rong-rian* โรงเรียน

sea *thá-le* ทะเล

seafood *aa-hǎan-thá-le* อาหารทะเล

search for *hǎa* หา

season *rúe-dou* ฤดู

seasoning, ingredient *khrûeang-prung* เครื่องปรุง

seat *thî-nâng* ที่นั่ง

see, *hěn* เห็น

sell *khǎay* ขาย

send *sòng* ส่ง

send an email *song-ii-meo* ส่งอีเมล์

September *kan-yaa-yon* กันยายน

seven *jèt* เจ็ด

several, many *lǎay* หลาย

sex, gender *phêt* เพศ

shampoo *yaa-sà-phǒm* ยาสระผม

shave *kon* โกน

she *khǎo* เขา

shelf/shelves *chán* ชั้น

ship, boat *ruea* เรือ

shoes *rawng-tháo* รองเท้า

shop, store *ráan* ร้าน

short (height) *tîa* เตี้ย

short (length) *sân* สั้น

shout *tà-kon* ตะโกน

shower, bath *àap-nám* อาบน้ำ

shrimp/prawn *kûng* กุ้ง

shut, close *pìt* ปิด

shy *aay, khîi-aay* อาย, ขี้อาย

siblings *phîi-nóng* พี่น้อง

sick, ill *mǎi-sà-baay* ไม่สบาย

sing *ráwng-phleng* ร้องเพลง

single (not married) *sòt* โสด

sink (in the bathroom) *àang-láang-nâa* อ่างล้างหน้า

sink (in the kitchen) *àang-láang-jaan* อ่างล้างจาน

sister (older) *phîi-sǎaw* พี่สาว

sister (younger) *náwng-sǎaw* น้องสาว

sit *nâng* นั่ง

six *hòk* หก

skilful *kèng* เก่ง

skinny *phǎwm* ผอม

skirt *krà-prong* กระโปรง

sleep *nawn* นอน

sleepy *ngûang-nawn* ง่วงนอน

slow, slowly *cháa* ช้า

small *lék* เล็ก

smart *chà-làat* ฉลาด

smile *yím* ยิ้ม

snack *khà-nǒm* ขนม

snake *ngou* งู

snow *hì-má* หิมะ

soap *sà-bòu* สบู่

socks *thǔng-tháo* ถุงเท้า

sofa *so-faa* โซฟา

soldier *thá-hǎan* ทหาร

son *lôuk-chaay* ลูกชาย

song *phleng* เพลง

sore, painful *jèp* เจ็บ

sorry (apology) *khǎw-thôt* ขอโทษ

sorry (regret) *sǐa-jai* เสียใจ

sour (taste) *prîaw* เปรี้ยว

spicy *phèt* เผ็ด

spoon *cháwn* ช้อน

stairs, steps *ban-dai* บันได

stand *yuen* ยืน

start, begin *rôem* เริ่ม

state *rát* รัฐ

sticky rice *khâaw-nǐaw* ข้าวเหนียว

stink *měn* เหม็น

stir-fry *phàt* ผัด

stop, halt *yùt* หยุด

stove *tao* เตา

straight ahead *trong-pai* ตรงไป

street, road *thà-nǒn* ถนน

strong *khǎeng-raeng* แข็งแรง

student (school) *nák-rian* นักเรียน

student (university) *nák-sùek-sǎa* นักศึกษา

study, learn *rian* เรียน

sugar *nám-taan* น้ำตาล

Sunday *wan-aa-thít* วันอาทิตย์

surname *naam-sà-kun* นามสกุล

sweep (the room) *kwàat-bâan* กวาดบ้าน

sweet *wǎan* หวาน

sweet, dessert *khǎwng-wǎan* ของหวาน

swim *wâay-nám* ว่ายน้ำ

T

table *tó* โต๊ะ

take off *thàwt* ถอด

talk *phôut, khuy* พูด

tall *sǒung* สูง

tasty *à-ròi* อร่อย

tea *chaa /nám-chaa* ชา/น้ำชา

teach *sǎwn* สอน

teacher *khrou* ครู

teeth, tooth *fan* ฟัน

telephone *tho-rá-sàp* โทรศัพท์

television *thii-wii* ทีวี

tell (someone) *bàwk* บอก

temple (Buddhist) *wàt* วัด

ten *sìp* สิบ

ten thousand *mùen* หมื่น

Thai *phaa-sǎa-thai* ภาษาไทย

Thailand *prà-thêt-thai* ประเทศไทย

thank; thank you *khàwp-khun* ขอบคุณ

that *nân, nán* นั่น, นั้น

then *láew-kâw* แล้วก็

there *thîi-nân* ที่นั่น

there is/there are *mii* มี

they *khǎo* เขา

thin *phǎwm* ผอม

think *khít* คิด

think of *khít-thǔeng* คิดถึง

thirsty *hǐw-nám* หิวน้ำ

this *nîi, nii* นี่, นี้

thousand *phan* พัน

three *sǎam* สาม

Thursday *wan-phá-rúe-hàt* วันพฤหัส

ticket *tǔa* ตั๋ว

time *we-laa* เวลา

tired, exhausted *nùeay* เหนื่อย

today *wan-níi* วันนี้

tofu *tâo-hôu* เต้าหู้

toilet *sûam* ส้วม

tomato *má-khŭea-thêt* มะเขือเทศ

tomorrow *prûng-níi* พรุ่งนี้

too, also *dûay* ด้วย

tooth, teeth *fan* ฟัน

toothbrush *praeng-sĭi-fan* แปรงสีฟัน

toothpaste *yaa-sĭi-fan* ยาสีฟัน

torch, flashlight *fai-chăay* ไฟฉาย

towel *phâa-chét-tua* ผ้าเช็ดตัว

town *mueang* เมือง

traffic jam *rót-tìt* รถติด

traffic light *fai-daeng* ไฟแดง

train *rót-fai* รถไฟ

train station *sà-thăa-nii-rót-fai* สถานีรถไฟ

tree *tôn-mái* ต้นไม้

trousers *kaang-keng* กางเกง

try on (clothes) *lawng* ลอง

Tuesday *wan-ang-khaan* วันอังคาร

turn left *líaw-sáay* เลี้ยวซ้าย

turn right *líaw-khwăa* เลี้ยวขวา

twelve *sìp-săwng* สิบสอง

twenty *yîi-sìp* ยี่สิบ

two *săwng* สอง

U

ugly *nâa-klìat* น่าเกลียด

umbrella *rôm* ร่ม

uncomfortable *mâi-sà-baay* ไม่สบาย

under, underneath *tâi* ใต้

understand *khâo-jai* เข้าใจ

university *má-hăa-wít-thá-yaa-lai* มหาวิทยาลัย

up *khûen* ขึ้น

upstairs *khâang-bon* ข้างบน

urgent *dùan* ด่วน

use *chái* ใช้

used to *khoei* เคย

usually *pà-kà-tì/pòk-kà-tì* ปกติ

V

vacant *wâang* ว่าง

vacation, holiday *wan-yùt* วันหยุด

van *rót-tôu* รถตู้

vegetable *phàk* ผัก

vegetarian *mang-sà-wí-rát* มังสวิรัติ

very *mâak* มาก

village *mòu-bâan* หมู่บ้าน

villager *chaaw-bâan* ชาวบ้าน

visit a doctor *pai-hăa-măw* ไปหาหมอ

visitor (guest) *khàek* แขก

voice, sound *sĭang* เสียง

vomit (verb) *aa-jian* อาเจียน

W

wait for *raw* รอ

wait a moment *raw-dĭew* รอเดี๋ยว

wake up *tùen-nawn* ตื่นนอน

walk *doen* เดิน

want *yàak-dâi* อยากได้

want to *tâwng-kaan* (formal) ต้องการ, *yàak* (informal) อยาก

warm (weather) *ùn* อุ่น

wash *láang* ล้าง

wash clothes *sák-phâa* ซักผ้า

wash dishes *láang-jaan* ล้างจาน

wash face *láang-nâa* ล้างหน้า

wash hair *sà-phŏm* สระผม

wash hands *láang-mue* ล้างมือ

watch (show, movie) *dou* ดู

water *nám* น้ำ

waterfall *nám-tòk* น้ำตก

we, us *rao* เรา

wear *sài* ใส่

weather *aa-kàat* อากาศ

wedding *ngaan-tàeng-ngaan* งานแต่งงาน

Wednesday *wan-pút* วันพุธ

week *aa-thít* อาทิตย์

weight *nám-nák* น้ำหนัก

well, good *dii, sà-baay-dii* ดี, สบายดี

well (skillfully) *kèng* เก่ง

well cooked, well done *sùk* สุก

wet *pìak* เปียก

what *à-rai* อะไร

what time *kìi-mong* กี่โมง

when *mûea-rài* เมื่อไร

where *thîi-nǎi* ที่ไหน

white *sǐi-khǎaw* สีขาว

why *tham-mai* ทำไม

wife *phan-rá-yaa* ภรรยา

win, *chá-ná* ชนะ

wind *lom* ลม

window *nâa-tàng* หน้าต่าง

winter *rúe-dou-nǎaw* ฤดูหนาว

withdraw (money) *thǎwn-ngoen* ถอนเงิน

woman, female *phôu-yǐng* ผู้หญิง

work, job *ngaan* งาน

work (verb) *tham-ngaan* ทำงาน

world *lôk* โลก

write *khǐan* เขียน

wrong (incorrect) *phìt* ผิด

Y

year *pii* ปี

yellow *sǐi-lǔeang* สีเหลือง

yes *châi* ใช่

yesterday *mûea-waan-níi* เมื่อวานนี้

you *khun* คุณ

younger brother *náwng-chaay* น้องชาย

younger sister *náwng-sǎaw* น้องสาว

your *khǎwng-khun* ของคุณ

Z

zebra *máa-laay* ม้าลาย

zero *sǔun* ศูนย์

zoo *sǔan-sàt* สวนสัตว์